THE GOOD LIFE LAB

[Pass it on!]

A GIFT FOR

....

....

....

....

....

....

THE GOOD LIFE LAB

Radical Experiments in Hands-On Living

WENDY JEHANARA TREMAYNE

Storey Publishing

*The mission of Storey Publishing is to serve our customers by
publishing practical information that encourages
personal independence in harmony with the environment.*

Edited by Pam Thompson and Carleen Madigan
Art direction and book design by Alethea Morrison
Cover illustrations by © Bert van Wijk (third panel), Grady McFerrin (inside front and back),
© Kristian Olson (bottom panel), © Meg Hunt (second panel), and © Melinda Beck (top panel)
Photography and interior illustration credits appear on page 318

STOREY PUBLISHING
210 MASS MoCA Way
North Adams, MA 01247
www.storey.com

Printed in China by R.R. Donnelley
10 9 8 7 6 5 4 3 2 1

Library of Congress Cataloging-in-Publication Data

Jehanara Tremayne, Wendy.
  The good life lab / by Wendy Jehanara Tremayne.
    pages cm
  Includes index.
  ISBN 978-1-61212-101-7 (pbk. : alk. paper)
  ISBN 978-1-60342-888-0 (ebook)
  1. Consumption (Economics) 2. Lifestyles. 3. Technological innovations—Social aspects.
  I. Title.
HC79.C6J44 2013
978.9'67—dc23
                      2012042977

Bismillah al rahman al rahim
In honor of Al Hayy

CONTENTS

Foreword(s), 11

Preface, 19

PART I: LIFE IMAGINED

Life in the Waste Stream. 26

Jump and the Net Will Appear. 32

Broken Heart Seeks Giant Band-Aid. 43

To Live a Decommodified Life 47

Everything Is a Tool to Change the World 52

Commodified People. 54

Swap-O-Rama-Rama 57

Nature Is the Truest Book 64

Ladybugs in New York City. 70

What Is the Cost of a Job?. 72

The Sky Is the Ocean. 75

PART II: LIFE HANDS ON

Makers of Shelter 82

Building in Truth or Consequences 93

Free Fuel 102

Things of Value 112

The Notorious Goblins 116

The Cost of Living 123

Take Time 128

Getting Better All the Time 131

Nature Unlocked 140

The Digital Homestead 157

The Least Useful Most Fun Thing 164

A Cottage Industry 166

Wisdom 177

PART III: LIFE LAB

Mad Skills 188

Kitchen Magic 217

Power, Electronics, and Technology 258

Cars and Fuel 274

Shelter 283

Holy Scrap 298

Epilogue: Make Mistakes 305

Resources, 308

Acknowledgments, 317

Credits, 318

If it is bread that you seek, you will have bread.
If it is the soul that you seek, you will find the soul.
If you understand this secret,
you know you are that which you seek.

— RUMI

FOREWORD(S)

THE MOST CREATIVE AND INNOVATIVE ADULTS I know are good at taking risks, learning new things, and immersing themselves in the tools and materials out of which they can make new things. When I founded *Make* magazine, I began calling them *makers* and soon I was considering just how different they are from those who only see themselves as consumers, not producers.

This book is all about becoming a maker. Making is an active mindset. It means you can learn to do anything you really want to learn. It doesn't mean you will be the best at it. The effort itself is worthwhile, even if all you gain is an appreciation of how much better others are at it than you. Makers understand the value of openness and the importance of sharing what you learn, especially from failure.

Making is an approach to doing things in spite of the fact that you don't know how they will turn out. Wendy writes: "Start even if you don't know how." That's a maker's reason for getting started. It is about having projects you want to do, knowing that you hope to learn something. The best projects are the most challenging. Making is exciting because you don't really know what you're getting yourself into. Inevitably, once you dive in, many unexpected things happen.

The Good Life Lab is not another predictable set of recipes encouraging you to do what others have done in hopes that it'll work for you. It is an invitation to experiment on your own and to try to live a life of your own making. It will be messy, imperfect, and a lot more fun. It will be your adventure.

— **Dale Dougherty,** founder of *Make* magazine

WENDY TREMAYNE IS A NEW KIND OF GENTLE, LOVING, PRACTICAL RADICAL. Writing with humor, lightness, and intelligence from a peaceful and compassionate place, she demonstrates how, following our heart's promptings and using the full resources of our bodies, minds, and souls, we can create a new life for ourselves, one in harmony with our true humanity, in service to our Earth, and attuned to the deeper realities of the cosmos. Wherever we live, whatever our situation in life, we can all learn something from Wendy's "radical experiments in hands-on living."

— **Christopher Bamford,** author of *An Endless Trace: The Passionate Pursuit of Wisdom in the West*

THE GOOD LIFE LAB IS A WONDERFUL, OPEN WINDOW inviting you into the radically common sense adventures of Wendy and Mikey. It's well worth going out of your way to look into it.

They show us how we can begin to practice transformative homesteading — the conscious habitation and improvement of our lives, land, and community — anywhere, starting right where we are, wherever we are. The key is to become aware of, engage with, then begin to work *with* the resources flowing through our lives (time, food, energy, joy, neighbors, shelter, "waste") in a way that simultaneously magnifies these and other resources and creates additional potentials, often by also enhancing others' capacity to do the same or better.

This is where I feel the true power of this book lies. It tells a story of striving, creating, and living in a way that elevates life beyond ourselves. It is not about an insular self-sufficiency, for Wendy and Mikey are not isolationists, but rather weavers of interconnecting webs. They seek out those in both their immediate physical community and the global digital community to teach them the skills they lack, while giving back with their growing strengths and the knowledge and creations that arise from their collaborative experimentation.

I love the mind- and soul-opening quotes that begin each section of this book, and how they lead into the tales of Wendy's and Mikey's experiences. These are stories within stories. The story of how they built their papercrete structures is also about how they scavenged the discarded paper for the papercrete, about the miscellaneous found and repurposed parts that made the tools to mix and apply the papercrete, about all the joyful, eccentric, sharing innovators they encountered along the way. Point to just about anything within their homestead, and the stories begin to flow. Not just any stories, but empowering adventure tales, with quirky twists and turns that go places you don't expect, for which you are grateful, because it shows how you might get there, too. As Wendy says, "It's all common sense — free and available to all."

— **Brad Lancaster,** author of *Rainwater Harvesting for Drylands and Beyond*

MANY PEOPLE IN OUR CONTEMPORARY CONSUMER SOCIETY, feeling dissatisfied and disgruntled with the jobs and lifestyles in which they find themselves, daydream about a better life, a life that more accurately reflects their values, and a better world they wish to help create. Wendy Tremayne was one of those people, until she and her partner, Mikey, left their 9-to-5 jobs behind and began a quest for something very different, what Wendy describes as an "uncommodified" or "post-consumer" life. This book is the story of their journey, which led them to a small town in New Mexico, and of their lives homesteading there.

Wendy relates their story with an infectious spirit of adventure. She acknowledges fears, paradoxes, and contradictions, and describes many of the things she has learned. In these pages you will find practical information to guide you through a remarkably varied range of do-it-yourself projects, including building with papercrete, plastic welding, and fermenting your own kombucha, kimchi, and tempeh. But far more compelling than the DIY skills themselves is Wendy's articulation of the values that have guided her and Mikey to learn these things.

No book, this one included, can offer step-by-step instructions for creating the life you dream of. Each of us is unique, with our own histories, desires, and dreams. We cannot follow in Wendy's footsteps, yet certain aspects of her journey may illuminate a path for us. In sharing and reflecting upon the discoveries she and Mikey have made and the life they have created for themselves, Wendy Tremayne provides us with much creative inspiration and food for thought on our own transformative journeys.

— **Sandor Ellix Katz,** author of *The Art of Fermentation*

THIS IS NO ORDINARY HOW-TO BOOK. Through the telling of stories and offering of practical advice, Wendy reminds us that, to whatever extent we allow ourselves, we are all master practitioners in our own Good Life Lab. The moment we begin to visualize ourselves there (is your Good Life Lab coat white, plaid, or sequined? Only one thing's for certain — it's made from something rescued from the waste stream), magic starts to happen. The trick is to start *now*, from wherever we may be....

This book invites the embracing of paradoxes. It's okay to be part of problems and part of solutions at the same time — cultivating awareness of what constitutes an inspiring, sustaining, meaningful choice is the goal. The more aware we become of the ways in which even the smallest decisions affect our own health and the health of those around us, the more empowered, connected, intuitive — and alive — we are.

The Good Life Lab is not only an excellent technical resource for the emerging homesteader, it's a call to action and a guidebook for anyone with a heart that's ready to be followed.

— **Alyce Santoro,** the Center for the Improbable and (Im)Permacultural Research

LIFE IS A SINGLE WHOLE. In the end, nothing in this world is separable from anything else. You and I are who we are because of everyone and everything that has come before us. And everyone and everything that comes after us will bear the trace of who we have been: what we have thought, what we have said, and what we have done. The past is our heritage, the future is our legacy, and the present is our moment of truth.

We have been born into a world that is fast-changing. Never have so many men and women lived upon the earth. Never have men and women taken so much from the earth. The planet is groaning under the strain of our demands. Glaciers are melting, rivers turning toxic, rubbish heaping up, species vanishing — all so that we may keep up a way of life that gives us happiness. But are we really happy?

Wendy Jehanara Tremayne and Mikey Sklar set out to find a state of happiness that could not be bought with dollar bills. They let go of the corporate ladder and planted their feet on solid ground. By trial and error, with faith and vision, they built a new life, a life of work and play and celebration under the vast desert sky. This fascinating book tells their story.

The dervishes of old were known for their patched robes. When their robes tore or wore out, rather than buying new ones, they patched the ones they had. In time, like Joseph's famous cloak, their robes became quilts of many colors. Wendy and Mikey have made the whole of their life a patchwork robe. For all with eyes to see, that priceless dervish robe is a manifest sign of the bounty that is forever.

— **Pir Zia Inayat-Khan,** president of the Sufi Order International

---

IN THIS END-AND-BEGINNING TIMES that we are quickly approaching, many of us will be lighting out for points unknown, where Tremayne's not-to-panic common sense and a willingness to work will slow us down and let us live. And many of us will stay in coastal cities, or in tornado alleys, or near nuke plants or fracked pipelines — and the lessons from this book will apply just as well.

Wendy Tremayne is a refractor. Her slowing down the problem of the temperature in a room makes that room offer up unexpected sensual experiences. The practical solution to temperature control becomes a garden of delights. Then our horizon shifts and we are startled — because we simply don't see (in what we mistake for dirty hard work) this panoply of experiences.

In our shopped-together life, we see what the products instruct us to see. Beyond the horizon of our products, beyond the city limits — out there in New Mexico with Wendy, we are taught to see a rough, simple life. In Wendy's hands, we discover that it is delightful, moral, whole. I can't think of a more important gift for us, as it becomes increasingly clear that consumer society has deadly consequences. Earthalujah!

— **The Reverend Billy,** the Church of Stop Shopping

THIS IS LESS A STORY ABOUT SOME RADICAL new way of living than that of our return to normal. It's not about going "off the grid" and living in isolation from society, but rather about returning to the interconnectedness and social values that have characterized humanity pretty much since there have been humans. The fact that learning real skills, developing competencies, and sharing them with others in a mutually beneficial, winnerless game should appear so alien to most of us attests to how far we've drifted from anything resembling a cooperative culture.

The moment of disconnect, as far as I have been able to tell, was the Renaissance. Though hailed as a rebirth of the oldest human values and the beginning of rationality, the industrial age, and what we think of as modernity, it was actually — or at the very least also — the dismantling of a peer-to-peer society in favor of a highly centralized one. Local, abundance-based currencies were outlawed in favor of the same kinds of debt- and scarcity-based currencies we use today. In order to transact with one another, people had to borrow the "coin of the realm" from the central treasury. Trading with one another meant becoming indebted to the bank.

Of course, most people had little to trade once "chartered monopolies" (what we now call corporations) were given exclusive province over one industry or another. Instead of creating and exchanging value with one another as humans, craftspeople went to work for bigger companies in the city, and received wages for their time. Over the next few centuries, assembly lines and mass production served to further disconnect workers from the value they created — all the while presenting a false rationale of greater efficiency. This efficiency was never real: unaccounted for in the equation are the public roads required to ship all this stuff from factories to towns, as well as the environmental costs of factory production. The only thing it did better was disconnect us from any sense of competency, self-sufficiency, or local value creation.

Luckily for us, that system is finally breaking down. Corporations have collected all the money by now, and they've lost the ability to create any more money with it. They are stuck improving their balance sheets by shedding assets and workers instead of making anything new. The resulting unemployment crisis is a blessing in disguise, requiring us to seek the kinds of solutions in this book.

Actually doing stuff may seem scary to those of us more familiar with meaningless cubicle activity than real value generation. It feels a bit like being thrown on a desert island and being forced to come up with a skill set worthy of membership in the tribe. As this book amply demonstrates, those skills are attainable, even innate. The readiness is all.

— **Doug Rushkoff,** author of *Life, Inc.* and *Present Shock*

preface

I am writing this book more than a half century after the publishing of
Helen and Scott Nearing's classic *Living the Good Life: How to Live
Sanely and Simply in a Troubled World* (1954). The world that they
found too brutal to remain a part of and chose to leave has hardly
become less troubled. A simple life is even harder to find today than it
was in 1932 when the Nearings left New York City to start a homestead in rural Vermont.

Like the Nearings, we began our journey in New York, where a
real estate agent and a package of ladybugs helped bring into focus one
thing: We were going to have to leave the city if we wanted to lead the
lives we dreamed about. My partner, Mikey, and I lusted for a life free
of pointless drudgery. We wanted to do meaningful work that contributed to life and did not have a detrimental cost to others. We believe
that the collective bounty of our planet — food, water, air, and shelter
— ought to be available to everyone, whatever their economic status,
and we wanted to be part of that vision. These ideals sound simple, but
they have not been easy to follow. Not for us, not for the Nearings, and
not for those inspired by their writings over the fifty-odd years between
their adventure and ours.

In the city, we fantasized about living closer to nature. We wondered if it was possible to secure healthy food and clean water. Since the
two of us had only lived in the suburbs and the city, Mikey and I had
plenty of acculturated knowledge. That is, we knew how a complex

society worked and how to work in it. What we craved was a more natural knowledge, a connection to nature and the rest of life. We tried to imagine a different sort of lifestyle, one less entangled with commerce, materialism, and the influences of marketing. The rewards of our fancy jobs, we saw, could never remedy what we felt was missing from our lives: time to develop our own creative ideas, participation in envisioning and shaping the world, and freedom from the exhausting work that we, along with many others, had become accustomed to. We wanted to explore what life could be in an environment free of at least some of the pressures of a monetary system and a society structured by capitalism. Recognizing that an economy based on both perpetual growth and limited resources makes no sense, we started asking ourselves what *could* be relied on. Contributing to the making of a different kind of economy seemed to us a reasonable thing to do. We never set out to prove that life could be lived *without* money, but we wanted to make our lives have less to do with it.

Our hunch was that it would not be long before the economic system crashed anyway, so we pulled our retirement savings out of the stock market and hedged a new and less popular bet. We bought resources: an acre of land and tools to make things.

Mikey and I had each other and a shared vision. We set out to make a life that freed us to create, explore, learn, play, eat, and live without too much compromise to our souls. We didn't know at the beginning just how wonderful a world it would be. Nor did we know how soon after we made our new commitments we would see the old world come crashing down. In retrospect, our timing was excellent.

Some of the techniques shared in this book are for people starting out in the commodified world. Without understanding the ways in which our commodified lives shaped us, we might have found ourselves thousands of miles from where we started but no different for having traveled there.

Once out in the desert of southern New Mexico, as makers of things, we learned the meaning of the saying that life is as interesting as your interest in it. As we moved away from consumer goods and services and learned to replace them with what we could make ourselves, we became interested in and better versed in many types of knowledge: biology, chemistry, botany, construction, physics, herbalism, and electronics, to name a few. We found ourselves doing everything from textile design to car repair. We came to this lifestyle with no special skills or talents — just a bit of courage, inspiration, and genuine curiosity. You can bet we made plenty of mistakes (and you're going to hear about some of them!), yet we were able to achieve most of what we'd set out to do. Today, we happily live on a homestead that we designed

The front door to our homestead is composed of scraps of metal from a shipping container and bits of rebar. The wall is made of paper mixed with cement and sealed with stucco. We made it in the shape of an arrow that points up, a reminder to imagine.

and constructed ourselves, grow and wildcraft our own food and medicine, make our own household goods and fuel, and produce our own power. Not because we're super talented, but because we're human beings, and human beings are inherently creative.

There is no such thing as an uncreative person. This is too easy to forget in our current economic system, in which consumers don't need to know very much. The less people know, the more finished goods they buy. Our current economic system doesn't encourage deep thinking, because that leads to seeing the enormity of the cost of the human labor and natural resources that bring us cheap goods. But as makers of things, your quality of life actually hinges on your understanding of the larger world, and so a deeper interest in life naturally blossoms along with your skills. Once you become a creator rather than a consumer, a wonderful discovery awaits: You are more than you may have thought yourself to be. By connecting to nature, Mikey and I began to see how our lives meet up with the life of this world. My biggest hope is that this book will point you toward the very same spot.

Mikey and I are hardly free of the commodified world. We rely on it still. We use technology to run our cottage industry and store-bought tools to build our homestead; we pump city water to our gardens and purchase readymade appliances. What changed is our thought process. We recognize compromises when we make them and strive to make better choices as our knowledge and skills advance. What we have to offer you is our story, process, and discoveries, along with the effect that our choices had on our lives. Creating a decommodified life is a life-long process. Perhaps one day we will hear your story along with new and better ways to meet the challenges we encounter.

I wouldn't claim that the lifestyle that Mikey and I chose is *the* way to live. It is *a* way to live. If we had kept our jobs and stayed a part of the mainstream economy, we would never have learned what we have. We wouldn't have had the time.

Our first paper dome survived monsoon season and met its first double rainbow.

Our story is likely different from yours. But perhaps it offers something useful to people who are on the brink of changing their own lives. Fundamental to all our stories is that lives are imagined before they come into being. We hope you will imagine something beautiful. If we make the best of this time, perhaps history will call it the start of a renaissance. We are the first people alive to witness the condition of the entire world being for sale. If we become makers of things, we become the revolutionaries of our age.

The lessons in this book are some of the most valuable lessons of my life. I offer them to you with the hope that what I learned can bring benefit to your life as well.

part 1

LIFE

IMAGINED

Life in the waste stream

Waste is a design flaw.
— KATE KREBS

I peed into a large green plastic cat-litter container that I keep in the bathroom. With its lid tightened, I carried the amber fluid outside and increased its volume by five times with water from a spigot that juts out from under the swamp cooler on the side of the house. (Swamp coolers are common in New Mexico. They use less power than air conditioners and work by putting a bit of humidity into the air.) I poured the diluted pee around a young sapling, thinking about the nitrogen in it.

No drinking water was flushed.

Some people call urine *liquid gold* because its value in nitrogen is greater than gold to life. I am happy to preserve all I can, and keep the waste I create on my 1-acre homestead. I try to do so with more than my pee.

In the kind of navy blue jumpsuit a gas station attendant wears, silk-screened with *Holy Scrap* on the back, Mikey was outside busying about a not-so-sturdy table in the yard. His jumpsuit was less stained than the white Dickies overalls I wore, which is typical for the two of us. Mikey labors only after strategizing ways to avoid labor, and he employs every possible machine before resorting to muscular effort. I growl my way through tasks on might and will until progress comes. His navy uniform reminded me of the Con Edison uniform he had worn to the office during his final days working for an investment bank. In prankster fashion, he had shown up to work in a variety of odd outfits: the Con Edison jumpsuit, a Chuck E. Cheese shirt complete with name-tag, and the uniform worn by employees of the sandwich franchise Subway. Wall Street was far away from us now, though Mikey solved life's problems with the same intensity that the Wall Street bank had once demanded of him.

Mikey circled the makeshift workbench to compare the contents of three jars marked with masking tape and Sharpie: CALICHE from south of town, RED CLAY from veins on our property, and MONTICELLO MUD from a rural community 60 miles away. Days earlier, he had mixed the clay samples with water and shook them hard before letting them settle. When they did, the clay and sand separated in bands. The sample with the highest clay-to-sand ratio stood out from the rest: the caliche was the winner. We'd use that as a substitute for a portion of the Portland cement used to make papercrete, the material we build domes out of, including a future guesthouse and a place to store the batteries of our photovoltaic (PV) solar array.

In many ways it was a typical day. Some of our vision was complete: a remodeled home, gardens, a flagstone patio that wrapped around a fire pit, and one earthy-looking dome. I imagined our acre as a temporary autonomous zone not smothered by civilization. A sign that once read ROBINA TRAILER PARK stood tall in the front of the lot, indicating a time when commerce took place here. My imagination transformed the sign into a giant metal flower that hung over the sidewalk out front to shade passersby from the harsh desert sun. For now the words were barely legible, covered in thin white paint. The flower would live in the realm of my imagination a bit longer. Permission to make non-utilitarian objects of beauty would come when the guesthouse dome was finished and the outdoor shower, shade structure, and workshop built.

Still, each day, bit by bit, living in the waste stream, we make manifest what our imaginations have already committed to memory.

I saved this wheelbarrow from the trash, welded the wheel casing back on, and used it to carry loads of rocks to build a fire pit.

To match my stained overalls, I wore a pair of ratty brandless sneakers that I picked up on bag day when a whole bag of thrift-shop loot was just five bucks. I'd replace my sneakers soon enough with another bag-day pair headed for the landfill.

Living in the waste stream feels to me like paying homage to materials already taken and energy already spent. Consider my tattered sneakers: the fuel used in their production, the machines built for their assembly, and the complex systems designed to distribute them. Imagine the people who participated in the processes: their commutes to work and back again, the children and pets who waited at home, the things they could have done instead, the phones answered, the sunsets missed. I *did* want a new pair of sneakers, but somehow squeezing every last bit of life out of the ones I already owned made the activities and resources they'd required seem less wasteful. The weight of this was heavier than my lust for new stuff. Extending the life of any thing is good manners.

I know that compared to industries, corporations, and governments, an individual is insignificant. In measurable terms my actions hardly matter. But feeling tiny does not have to end at *why bother*. Feeling tiny does not dampen my desire to uphold a standard of waste etiquette. Caring and respect for life always stave off helplessness.

I grabbed an impact drill and attached another scrap of 2 by 10 that I'd pulled from a dumpster to a break in the garden bed. Nothing purchased, not this time.

My life's rhythm of moving things from the category of waste to the category of use has a tempo I enjoy. Each transformation produces a tangible result: a fence for privacy, a bed in the garden, a patio, a swinging gate, a shade canopy. They make our lives better. Every day I express gratitude for the labor that made my heart expand and pump blood through my veins, my muscles awaken and grow, and my bones lubricate in their joints. I remember the atrophy I felt sitting in a cubicle in a New York City skyscraper and the desire in my cells to use myself differently.

Waste liberates me from fashion, and I celebrate that emancipation every day. I am surprised at how relieved I feel each time I put on the same white Dickies overalls. From time to time, Mikey finds me in the yard to say, "Look — I dressed myself!" and spins before me to show the textile wonder he has put together, a hodgepodge of unmatched textures and colors gathered at clothing swaps and thrift stores. Our clothing wears the signs of our labor: stained, torn, and burned, each piece is a reminder that we have chosen a life in which labor and leisure are intimately connected. Every stain or tear contains a story, a moment that we treasured on our adventure.

The junky vehicles parked in our yard are of a piece with the rest: a dented pickup truck, a car that we nicknamed Chance that runs on waste vegetable oil (WVO), a biofuel-burning Beetle, and a little electric car that we bartered for. They require the legal minimum in insurance. If someone stole one of them or if a car got more dents, it would not touch my life very much. Value in an abundant life is different from value in a wealthy life: this abundance comes with freedom from worry.

When the small hot springs spa hotel across the street removed a wooden fence that had been standing in place for decades, the wood was thinned, boards were missing, and no hint of paint was left. The desert's dry heat had eaten up the wood's density, leaving 6-foot by 8-foot sheets of fence as light as cardboard. Noticing the dismantled fence, Mikey and I crossed the street to grab the obtainium. That's a word coined by Chris Hackett, the owner of the Brooklyn metal shop where I learned to weld. Obtainium is the prize found in the waste stream.

We grabbed the lightweight bounty and put it up behind our garden, where it closed off the rear of our property. "Perfect!" we said to each other with a smile of satisfaction. Nothing was purchased, no cycles kicked off. Another gift.

Sunday evenings we peruse alley dumpsters in our electric car. On Tuesdays, Mikey picks up WVO from a local restaurant and filters it at home by pouring it through the legs of jeans given to us by a local thrift shop because they were too dirty or torn to sell. Then he fuels two of our cars with the golden liquid and keeps some for solvent and stain. From the restaurant, he also grabs empty wine and beer bottles. Some we crush to make a nonwicking foundation for our buildings. Others we repurpose into flooring or use to make bottle windows in our domes. The rest we clean and refill with homemade wine, mead, or kombucha (a nutritional beverage — see page 238).

When we are actively building, we visit the recycling center weekly to fill our Toyota's flatbed with newspaper and cardboard that we use for making pulpy papercrete insulation, garden liners, or any number of things. Throughout the year we pick up free mulch from the town's tree trimmings.

Spring is the season for our annual pilgrimage to a nearly 3,000-pound camel named Stanley. When we arrive, Carol, the love of Stanley's life, instructs her doting husband to use his front loader to fill our truck bed with Stanley's poo. Stanley jumps up and down, an impressive gesture for an animal who weighs more than a Honda I once drove across the country. Stanley shows our dog Sesame, Mikey, and me that he is happy about our having come to visit. We give his mama three bucks for a dozen eggs, wave hello to the pet ostrich kept around to eat the rattlesnakes, and head home to shovel shit for our garden with surprising joy.

Mikey and I consider ourselves gleaners. We're not unlike the microorganisms that clean the marrow from the bones left by the turkey vultures that pick through what's left behind by the coyotes that live across the Rio Grande. In nature everything has its place. Nothing wasted.

This load of camel poo is valuable. With a little compost and sand, it'll make a fine soil for our garden.

Jump and the Net Will Appear

Nothing can stop an idea whose time has come.
— Victor Hugo

Mikey and I are not native New Mexicans. We're city folks. At least we were until a few things happened that triggered an insatiable craving for something different from what the city offered us. Before we bought an acre of land and started living out of the waste stream, we lived in Brooklyn. Our lifestyle had a lot to do with our careers. We bought new goods and contributed to the waste stream. In New York we assembled a strange puzzle, searching for why we felt incomplete. Then we asked ourselves what we were going to do about it. We had never lived in any world but the one that we began to call the *default world*. Our default world had demanding jobs, crazy commutes, debt, limited free time, and other things that we learned to see as compromises to our happiness. We looked at these things anew and from odd angles, and then made unusual decisions.

When I learned to reclaim my creativity and use it to make a world of my own envisioning, things got really exciting and everything seemed possible. Even a quirky, junk-made, off-grid homestead in New Mexico and an abundant life without a standard job.

In the spring of 2001, I quit my job right after I had courted a cigarette company. I caught a glimpse of how dangerous the skills of my profession could be when I crafted a crop circle media campaign for the company. My idea was that real crop circles would be made and photographed, and the pictures leaked to the press. The designs would mimic the corporation's logo, obscuring it just enough that the media would believe the contrived crop circles to be real and report them to an unassuming public. Once the press spread the image far and wide, and after the corporation attained hundreds of thousands of dollars' worth of free advertising, I would advise the cigarette company to accept credit for the prank. Yikes. If I was going to wield mojo, it ought to be for better ends than this.

So in what seemed like a midlife crisis, I unburdened myself of the title Creative Director of Green Galactic. I was immediately relieved. I would not have to hype another DJ, schmooze another writer, promote another plastic widget, or make another famous person more famous. I would never sucker the public into studying a cigarette company's logo without realizing it.

It would not have mattered if I were a nurse, an electrician, a librarian, or a photographer. I had already been an employee of Burger King, a graphic designer, a bassist, and a maid before settling into a career in marketing. Every job had come with heavy compromises. Why? My hunch was that it had something to do with money.

I hit the road in my metallic gold Honda to try to figure out what I should do. I knew I risked finding it impossible to return to life as I had known it. But continuing in my current course seemed harder than taking a chance.

First, I headed to Nevada, lured by a discovery I had made a year earlier of a 1.5-mile diameter wonder world called Black Rock City. It's thrown up each year in the Nevada desert for the Burning Man festival. The next festival was months away, but I planned to volunteer at 80 Acres, the year-round site for storage and the building of Black Rock City's infrastructure. I wanted to give something back to the community that a year earlier had helped me find permission to seek a new way of life.

At first when I discovered Burning Man, I had a hard time believing that for over a decade people had been building Black Rock City, making pilgrimage to it, and deconstructing it. I wished I had known. At times, the temporary city had contained 40 radio stations, two daily newspapers, a post office with its own zip code, several hair salons, a roller rink, an opera, an ice-cream truck, an airport, and many other desired things. I approached it shyly at first, unable to fathom that the whole city was built for the giving of gifts, that its economy is a *gift economy*.

It was the discovery of the gift economy that untethered me from my idea of myself. That's what happens when you catch a glimpse of something important. You can't pretend you didn't see it.

You have to move forward and find out what it wants from you.

People climb Star Seed, an installation by New York City–based artist Kate Raudenbush, during an intense dust storm at Burning Man 2012.

Burning Man, you may have heard, is a lot of things to a lot of people. I was drawn in by the large-scale art that required miles of open desert and reached the height of city buildings. Nowhere else had I seen seasoned career artists given equal space and equal billing with first-timers. It seemed fair. Many times throughout my career I had watched creative people with the money to hire publicity and marketing teams advance successful careers while artists with more talent and less money blurred into the background. The business of art is anything but fair. But in Black Rock City, the only way to achieve social rank was to make something and what contained the greatest value was given away. A gift.

In a gift economy a gift must always move. If it is kept something of similar value must move on instead. If it becomes property it perishes.

— Lewis Hyde, from *The Gift*

In a gift economy, value is found in people and not in things. People who are in the know give their gift. The recipients do not at first realize that their end of the stick is the shorter one — not until they themselves give, which is a natural reaction to having been given to. Then they arrive at the secret destination and seek out a recipient for their gift, knowing that they have become the new treasure holders. If the giving were to stop, if everyone suddenly were to hoard, the value of the entire city would be reduced to nil — bankrupt! But the giving doesn't stop. Life in Black Rock City is more abundant than life in the default world. There, giving is infectious and even competitive.

I understand that there were real reasons why the seemingly ideal way of life in Black Rock City existed only one week out of the year. The material the city was built from and everything in it was produced under

Gift Ec[onomy]

OPEN SOUR[CE] HARDWARE: SHARES knowledge by making all the design files of a project available so that it can easily be fixed, modified & built upon by ANYONE

SUSTAINING & RECEIVING SUSTENANCE FROM NATURE: OUR BIRTHRIGHT

BLOGS & VIDEOS: WAYS TO SHARE KNOWLEDGE WITH THE LARGER COMMUNITY

BARTERING: A NON-MONETARY FORM OF CURRENCY (IS TAXABLE IN THE U.S.)

SKILL-SHARING PARTIES: FUN & SOCIAL WAYS TO SHARE WHAT YOU HAVE LEARNED WITH A LOCAL COMMUNITY

A GIFT IS A THING WE DO NOT [earn]

EFFORTS IT IS BESTOWED UPO[N] US

GIFTING OF A GIFT TENDS TO ESTABLISH

THE COMMONS: RESODURCES (SHARED) AMONG COMMUNITIES; for example, CREATIVE COMMONS IS A NON-PROFIT ORGANIZATION THAT OFFERS A WAY TO KEEP CREATIVE WORKS AVAILABLE FOR (OTHERS) TO BUILD UPON & (SHARE)

FEEDING PEOPLE: (CREATES JOY!)

COPYLEFT LICENSES: ASSURE THAT _YOUR_ GOOD IDEA & ALL IT SPARKS WILL REMAIN (FREE) AFTER YOU RELEASE IT INTO THE WORLD

FREE BOXES & JUNK PILES: PUBLIC SPOTS WHERE PEOPLE PLACE (STILL USABLE) GOODS & OFFER THEM UP FOR "FREE"

FILE SHARING: DISTRIBUTES & PROVIDES ACCESS TO DIGITALLY STORED MATERIAL SO THAT IT MAY BE (SHARED)

onomy

T BY OUR OWN

like THE SALE of A COMMODITY, THE LATIONSHIP BETWEEN THE PARTIES INVOLVED...."

— Lewis Hyde

the weight of capitalism and paid for with money earned by the same people who went to the desert to escape money. People with impressive careers and good salaries pioneered the gift economy. Each year they made the pilgrimage to Black Rock City as if to set free something that was all but lost. Like a snake eating its tail, Burning Man, a paradox, was the by-product of capitalism, a response to it, and, if one but knew how to look at it, perhaps its cure.

It was living in Black Rock's gift economy that caused me to press my life's reset button, quit my job, and hit the road to try to piece together what had happened.

I should have known better than to volunteer at 80 Acres. People out there bend hot metal wearing garden gloves. Rosie, a metal artist from New York who had moved to San Francisco, was the right type. Rosie confidently exhibited a 4-inch-long, three-dimensional scar that marked the spot where an out-of-control welder had nearly met her jugular vein — while she was building a 100-foot-diameter chandelier for Burning Man. She had classic Burning Man appeal: she was knowledgeable, creative, independent, and fearless. Some part of me wanted to be as self-assured as Rosie. Another part naively believed that I already was as tough as she was. That's how I messed up my hip, trying to pick up a railroad tie. After the railroad tie incident, the manager of 80 Acres, a surly old guy who could easily have been mistaken for a pirate, told me I'd better "go git" to the doctor. Defeated, I drove my Honda 500 miles south, using only my left foot to control the pedals of the car. In Los Angeles I met up with a helpful friend who took me to the doctor.

Days later I signed a hospital release form, bought a set of crutches, and drove left-footed out of the hospital parking lot. I left behind the ready-and-waiting surgeon who had hoped to have a go at my hip's repair. Being on a road trip allowed me to believe my imagination to be mightier than my mind. I placed a risky bet on my own strong will rather than a surgeon's hand. Besides, he'd be there later if I needed him. I had heard stories about people who used yoga to work through physical difficulties. I was willing to try anything to avoid the surgeon's table. It was a winning bet. Yoga worked. In a few weeks, I kicked the crutches. Recognizing the treasure that I'd found, I made a promise to begin a lifelong yoga practice. To ensure that I would never forget the significance of the treasure, I decided to become a yoga teacher one day.

Since volunteering at 80 Acres was no longer an option, I spent the next four months on the road reviewing the decisions that had led me to quit my job.

It is no sign of wellness to be well adjusted to a sick society.
— Krishnamurti

Driving on Highway 1, I remembered taking a crappy job just to obtain medical benefits. *There were always good reasons for making bad decisions*, I said aloud to a 4-inch plastic troll that I had mounted to the dashboard with a glob of glue. My plastic patron saint came from a thrift shop in Topanga Canyon. She made a good road companion. Her hair was burned in spots, and melted wax covered her toes. We'd both been through something. My homely idol had skirted getting whisked away and dumped into the landfill by capturing the interest of a Topanga Canyon shopkeeper and then my own. An excellent listener and devoid of judgment, she welcomed the few words that broke the silence that I was learning to love.

On a moonless night in front of a cave on a beach in Southern California, green phosphorescent waves illuminated a black ocean. Gazing out, I remembered lying for several employers. It felt awful, but I had done it anyway. "Didn't everyone?" I asked the troll that I unstuck from the dashboard and placed in the sand next to me. With a candle lit by her side, she cast eerie shadows on the earthen wall at our backs.

In Moab, Utah, under a blanket of stars that seemed to multiply every hour, I remembered my first job offer after I got my bachelor's degree. I turned it down, even though it came from Grey, a top advertising agency. I couldn't survive on the $14,000 they offered me. I had loans to pay. Instead I moved into the future, head hung low, to meet an unknown fate that expressed itself through a string of featureless gigs: promotion manager for an engineering company that made multimeters, sales-team manager for a company that sold devices for attaching tags to garments, and promoter of magazines (including one for ham radio operators).

While cruising pristine Amish country in Pennsylvania, I remembered times I had compromised my better instincts. In college, knowing that no financial support was waiting for me after graduation, I turned away from art and chose instead to major in marketing, with a minor in business. It was a practical decision. I had student loans to pay back, and living in New York was going to be tough.

The Indian spiritual text the Bhagavad Gita says in words different from these that it is better to do a crappy job at what you alone are able to do (*your purpose*) than to do a great job at what someone else is here to do. This felt like an appropriate description for the predicament I was in. I wondered what I was meant to do.

Free of the cloak of my career, my ego regularly prompted me to think about the hole left behind by the part of my identity that I shed. It wanted to know who I was to become.

That would take time.

Your task is not to seek love, but merely to seek and find all the barriers within yourself that you have built against it.

— Rumi

My journey concluded with a return to Burning Man to live in Black Rock City's gift economy a second time. Then I headed home to learn what it means to be a yogi. Yoga studios were not yet as common as pizza joints. I searched out a seasoned, eccentric French yoga teacher and started an apprenticeship.

Four hours after I returned to the city, the World Trade Center towers disappeared from New York's skyline. I made my first pledge.

 I will no longer make decisions based on money.

Many of my friends thought I'd lost my mind when I told them I was becoming a yoga teacher. A few months earlier, as part of my midlife fire sale, I had given up what some would say was a perfectly good career. I was earning a good salary. I had medical insurance and a nice office in Brooklyn. I enjoyed my clients, who were mostly artists, filmmakers, authors, and musicians. For a while I thought this was all that I needed to be happy. But being unemployed and on the open road gave me time and space to review my choice of careers. Being the creative director of a pop culture marketing company was a reflection of my own desire to *be* creative. By which I don't mean the kind of creativity that shapes people and their ideas into products and advertising campaigns. The truth was, my job was unable to provide the substance that my heart demanded.

Giving this up to scrape by teaching yoga suddenly seemed perfectly reasonable. But old habits are hard to break. I was prewired to turn ideas into profit. I considered starting a yoga business. After all, I had more business experience than yoga experience. Doing so required opening a studio, managing other people, taking on debt, doing accounting, and essentially becoming more like the person I was trying to shed. I found the cycle of business that necessarily followed every good idea tiring and bland. The gift economy I had encountered at Burning Man had me wanting a skill that could be bartered, gifted, or exchanged for money. But in the default culture I'd been living in, to want a moderate amount of anything was practically a personal flaw, a weakness. Not wanting money did not jibe with the American way. I wondered why everything had to scale up in order to survive.

Life is long, I repeated to myself often, to settle the rising feeling that I had to know what I was going to do in the future *right away*. It was a habit left from keeping pace in the sped-up world of business.

In the four months that I spent on the road, I cried into 11,000 miles of American landscape and reviewed 33 years of life. I admit that I was a little disappointed when the trip was over and I pulled into New York in my Honda, not knowing anything more about what to do with my life than I knew when I had left. I did discover a few gems: yoga, silence, a taste of freedom, and a bit of courage.

Teaching yoga would have to carry me to whatever was next. To uphold the value of the gift, once I became a certified yoga teacher, I offered yoga classes with the clause *No one turned away for lack of funds*. I accepted barter and gifts as well as money. It was a start.

broken Heart seeks Giant Band-Aid

The lightning spark of thought generated in the solitary mind
awakens its likeness in another mind.

— THOMAS CARLYLE

"Are you a broken heart? I'm a Band-Aid!" said the guy standing in front me wearing a large floppy Band-Aid drawn in green and blue illuminated wire. Like a beauty queen's sash, the giant Band-Aid began at his right hip, crossed his chest, flopped over his left shoulder, and continued down his back.

"Yes," I said. "I am a broken heart." I was wearing an illuminated wire heart that throbbed with red light and hung at the center of my chest.

The Festival of the Hurting was a costume party put on by a group of metal artists in response to the disorientation New Yorkers felt in the aftermath of September 11. A Brooklyn warehouse was filled with amusement-park rides designed to injure those who rode them — not horribly, just a little. Flirtatious guys and girls dressed as nurses (but with thigh-high fishnet stockings) and folks with both real and imagined injuries relished the act of dressing one another's wounds. A real boy-meets-girl mixer.

I walked Mikey — a.k.a. Band-Aid Boy — over to a 20-foot-long teeter-totter set parallel to the ground. Step stools on each end waited for the next riders. I pointed. He hoisted himself up and onto the device. I got on the other end and immediately hunkered down with a squinted face and fists held tight, believing that I could, by effort, increase my body weight and become heavier than he. As if by will, I sent his end of the teeter-totter up into the air and pinned him to the ceiling at an uncomfortable height. He looked down at me, half excited and half scared to death.

The next morning I opened my apartment door to find Band-Aid Boy with a skateboard under one arm and an echinacea plant in his free hand.

"How'd you find my apartment?"

Mikey recited the string of actions he had performed to bring him to my stoop. There was basic reasoning and practical logic to start, but also the writing of computer code, searching community lists for posts with my name on it and clues as to who I was, and finally a good guess that of the two Wendys his research produced, the one who lived on Sackett Street was the one he'd met the night before. Brooklyn boasts only a few locations where dirt and a yard are possible, and I had told him that I was thinking about starting a garden. The Carroll Gardens brownstone I shared with a roommate was in a part of Brooklyn known for having backyards.

"Good guess," I said as I opened the door to let him in.

Days later I visited Mikey's apartment on Houston Street, where I found him working on the creation of a dozen pairs of men's and women's underwear. Each featured a pocket that held in place a small motor that could be turned on and off with a remote-control device he had built. Mikey *is* a lover of mischief and always clever. He, too, had discovered Burning Man and was planning to return with his new invention. His plan was to give out panties and then mix up the remotes and give them to people other than the ones who had received the underwear. "Panty Tag," he said, looking up from his soldering iron, lifting up a huge pair of magnifying glasses attached to his head, and flashing his mischievous smile.

Our first date. I found Mikey soldering together a dozen pair of motorized underwear.

Under my arm I carried a blanket that I was making for the desert pilgrimage. The blanket had two giant sets of arms: one for the person wearing the blanket so he or she could reach out into the world and the other for someone outside of the blanket who wished to reach in. "It's for spooning," I told him.

Burning Man was a few months away, and those who planned to attend were working like Christmas elves, making weird versions of the goods used in what I was coming to think of as the default world. Burning Man gave those who craved creativity a venue and a reason to make wacky versions of familiar things.

Our third date took place at the Madagascar Institute, a metal shop run by the artists who had produced the costume party. There I taught Mikey how to cut images into a 50-gallon metal drum using an oxy-acetylene torch, a skill I had acquired only weeks before. The images illuminated when a fire was burned inside the barrels. Mikey helped me complete the image of a tree with branches that morphed into the face of a woman with outstretched arms. On the back of the cylinder, we carefully cut the initials NYPD and FDNY, for the New York police and fire departments. The barrels were part of a public art project to honor the September 11 rescue workers.

Weeks later, with the city's permission, we placed the decorative metal barrels along the West Side Highway on a pedestrian walkway. In the belly of the drums, fires burned and lured New Yorkers from their apartments. Some who came chatted by the warmth of the fire. Others were more contemplative. I imagined the flames burning up what hurt too much to say.

Inspired by Burning Man's culture of makers, I acquired skills that turned my inclination from humdrum to curious. Mikey taught me to wire LED lights. I taught him to weld. We built a pair of bikes part by part, greasing each ball bearing and truing the spokes. For the first 263 days of our knowing each other (he counted), we made things.

Learning to weld and cut metal changed my life. Out in the desert the skill comes in handy all the time.

Broken Heart Seeks Giant Band-Aid

To Live a Decommodified Life

The desire to consume is a kind of lust. We long to have the
world flow through us like air or food. We are thirsty and hungry
for something that can only be carried in our bodies. Consumer
goods merely bait that lust, they do not satisfy it.
— LEWIS HYDE, FROM *The Gift: The Erotic Life of Property*

In 2002 the underground art community in New York City blossomed
and grew. In a given week one could learn to sew and make a furry
bear suit, learn about Central Park's edible plants, find out how to read
a schematic, learn the Hawaiian fire art called poi, solder, or go on an
unsanctioned historical tour of underground subway stations no longer
in use.

Consumerism and money were themes that popped up regularly
in creative projects. Performance artist Reverend Billy founded the
Church of Stop Shopping. With a real choir preaching the pitfalls of
materialism, Reverend Billy and his followers performed in churches
around the city, then the country, and then the world. The Billionaires
for Bush were regularly seen around town dressed in tuxedos and fancy
gowns. In character, they argued for the rights of the wealthy: to tax,
to maximize profit, to increase power. I added my own contribution to
the theme by creating a project called *The Vomitorium: Make Room
For More!*, a theatrical production modeled after the opulent parties
of the Roman Empire, where guests infamously engaged in consuming
astounding amounts of food, vomiting, and gorging themselves again

and again. The play invited reflection on the fate that eventually befell the Roman Empire.

It was a time of self-expression and self-reflection. Burning Man's gift economy and its DIY ethos were shaping a culture back at home. This culture helped Mikey and me recognize how commodified our lives were.

We realized that instead of making the goods we needed to live, we bought them. We chose what to buy by copying others or by listening to advertisements. Wearing branded clothing, we were ourselves walking advertisements. Since we didn't make things, we also didn't understand how things worked. If something broke, we threw it in the trash. We were not privy to information that might lead to responsibility. We didn't know which fibers and materials decomposed back into the earth or what toll the production of goods took on the planet. This information did not come on care labels along with the washing instructions or in owner manuals paired with gadgets. We had never considered that most of civilization was made out of petroleum and corn. Both can be abstracted and turned into a plethora of forms. Petroleum is turned into plastics and synthetic fibers that are then used to make consumer goods. It is also turned into fertilizers used to grow industrialized food. Living in the city, a place defined by its reliance on goods produced elsewhere, we consumed things with a cost that could be measured in petroleum, in both the delivery and production of goods. And we learned that the processed food we ate, which took varied forms from sweeteners to fiber, was actually modified corn. Animal products like meat and dairy we learned to view as corn products because animals not meant to consume corn were being raised on it at industrialized farms.

Our life cycle was a patterned loop of working to earn money to buy what we could have made ourselves — better and more responsibly. Our creativity, our most precious gift, we traded for money. The results of our labor hardly contributed to making the life of the earth any better. Deep down, we felt this.

With newly opened eyes we watched the same food supply trucks pull up behind all sorts of restaurants. "It's all the same," we said to each other while watching the same truck deliver to a run-down deli and then a fancy health food café across the street.

Documentaries about genetically modified organisms (GMOs), pesticides, and factory farming practices encouraged us to become food aware. We memorized the categories of goods that contained GMOs and avoided them. At the time the list consisted of cotton, corn, canola, and soy. Today the list is longer and harder to memorize.

We dumped our televisions and turned to online news sources. We started making more of our goods ourselves. Instead of buying new things, we favored what could be trash-picked. We modified junk to fulfill our needs. Changes in habit helped us see the relationship between our choices and the world. We avoided participating in sweatshop and child labor, pollution, and the abuse of resources worldwide by not consuming and by living out of the waste stream.

We started taking note of the things people did to reward themselves for the hard work they gave to their careers. They were things that Mikey and I had rewarded ourselves with all the time. Once out of our office cubicles, we had run off to fancy dinners and bought consumer goods and designer clothing.

I held on to the pledge that I had made a year earlier after months on the road. With Mikey, I added a promise.

We will search for an uncommodified life.

Make it Yourself Make it Better

Our life cycle was a patterned loop of working to earn money to buy what we could have made ourselves — better and more responsibly

Toothpaste

2 tablespoons
baking soda

+

pinch of
salt

+

1 tablespoon glycerin
(optional)

+

1 teaspoon
Dr Bronners
peppermint

Shake
well.

Hair Conditioner

Boil water equal to half
your container's volume

+

Steep yucca — or any
saponin-containing
local plant with 1/4 cup
rosemary and
2 tablespoons hibiscus

+

Strain and pour
into your container

Fill the rest of the container
with white vinegar.

All-Purpose Cleaner

A couple drops tea tree oil

A few drops of liquid castile soap

Pour this mixture into a jar

Mix 1 tablespoon Borax and 1 teaspoon baking soda in 2 cups warm water

Use soapberries in a muslin bag as laundry detergent

Dry loofa plants into sponges

Glass Cleaner

Mix 1/2 cup vinegar with enough purified water to fill your spray bottle

Add 3 drops of essential oil

Reuse your containers!

Everything Is a Tool to Change the World

Courage is not the absence of fear, but rather the judgment that
something else is more important than one's fear.

— Ambrose Redmoon

As I scraped by teaching yoga and doing freelance PR, my savings
dwindled. Was it sane to think I could live an uncommodified life in a
commodified world? Then I realized that my job had armed me with
useful skills. I knew how to engage the media and produce events. I
decided to use these skills to produce an event giving peace a voice.

Standing under a bridge in Central Park at not quite 7 a.m., I
watched the biggest snowstorm in decades dump white powder. Bare-
naked tree trunks that seemed drawn in charcoal swayed against the
backdrop of white and gray.

I knew that if I didn't take off all my clothes and dart out naked
into the snow, none of the volunteers who had followed me there would
either. I bolted. I let my still-warm, blood-filled body cut through the
sideways-falling crystals. When I reached Bethesda Fountain and looked
up toward the bronze Angel of Waters perched high in the air, I imagined that her outstretched arm beckoned me. I slowed my pace in front
of her and the four small cherubim standing below her: Health, Purity,
Temperance, and Peace. Nearby, a plaque, now covered in snow, had
been mounted to honor veterans of the world wars. In 41 days, America
would go to war with Iraq for the second time. We were in Central Park
to tell the world that we did not agree with that plan.

A high-pitched sound grew in volume. It was the other women, who, upon seeing me dart out from the bridge, followed. Their red-splotched naked bodies were coming my way. In less than three minutes we spelled out NO bUSH with our bodies. The snow felt hot on my back as I lay in my spot in the S. I stared up at the snowflakes falling on my face. I was broke, unemployed, and out in the middle of a snowstorm doing something kind of scary and kind of magical.

I wasn't just expressing my objection to the war that day. I was taking back the skills that I had given to industry, and by doing so I was redeeming myself. I had wanted to become an artist and had instead chosen marketing as a major in college — because it seemed the safe road. Years later, I found myself without artistic skill, at least in the traditional and commodified sense. I didn't paint or sculpt. I had not apprenticed in an art form. I had nothing to sell or hang in a gallery. I'd never had time for art as a hobby. I had gone from full-time student to full-time employee. Producing NO bUSH showed me that the skills I had learned over the course of my career could be themselves artistic, and they could be put to better ends. *Anything* can be used as a tool to transform the world.

Within days, images created by other groups spelled out messages that were broadcast back to us through the media. People in Hong Kong, Milan, Texas, Paris, Sydney, South Africa, Hiroshima, Cuba, Spain, New Zealand, Cape Town, Antarctica, and other places across the world spelled LOVE, SOS, No War; they drew hearts and peace signs with their bodies. From the Middle East came *salam*, peace in Arabic. I was satisfied as I had never been in my previous career. I felt useful.

I hereby give myself permission to be illogical, contradictory, crazy, and strange — whatever it takes to find a meaningful way to be in the world.

commodified people

> We've got the same genes. We're more or less the same. But our nature, the nature of humans, allows all kinds of behavior. I mean every one of us under some circumstances could be a gas chamber attendant and a saint.
>
> — NOAM CHOMSKY

Some time later, when my friend Marina and I emerged from the subway, we were swallowed up in a crowd. Cops and protesters mingled with people in business suits going to and from skyscraper offices; there were cops on bikes, reporters, and a clown wearing a rainbow wig. It was probably the worst day to be picking up a friend from out of town in midtown Manhattan. There were protests all over New York that summer, and it was hard to avoid running into them. In spite of the crowd, we managed to find our friend Ben, who had just flown in from New Orleans, and we headed to the subway station a block away. A few feet short of the station's entrance at Bryant Park, walking traffic slowed and then stopped. There was a commotion and an elevation of energy, some yelling, and fast movement. Some people standing next to me put their arms in the air and made peace signs with their hands. Our trio plus one piece of wheeled luggage dropped to the ground in response to a cop shouting, "Get down! Everybody get down!"

Police in riot gear stood shoulder to shoulder, holding orange nets up to their chins. Ben, Marina, and I, along with about 50 other people I'd never seen before, were encircled. Trapped. One by one, cops pushed those captured inside the net over the edge of it, face forward, hands held behind our backs by uniformed police. Noses were bloodied as people hit the pavement too fast and face-first. I was cuffed tight and put on a city bus that had been taken over by the NYPD. It delivered me to a temporary jail built for this occasion.

I learned that the old bus terminal on Pier 57 on the West Side had been converted to a makeshift jail weeks before the Republican National Convention. Inside the terminal I was stripped of my possessions, ID, phone, money, and joy and pushed into a cell with 50 or so other women and a 12-foot-long bench. I was in jail. Not for any protest, but just for being on a New York City sidewalk at the wrong time.

In jail the only water offered came out of black greased pipes sticking out of old rusty fountains protruding from the peeling cinderblock cell walls. While many did not pause over the water, I worried about my kidney infection. I'd left my antibiotics at home. How would I maintain the regimen of ten 8-ounce glasses of water a day that my doctor had advised? *I'm going to die in this place*, I thought as I watched others sip the water.

The next day the group was bused to a real jail in downtown Manhattan. On the way a college student had a genuine panic attack. Crying, screaming, and panting for breath, she was dragged from her seat and chained to a metal pole that divided the bus as though this shift in position would calm her down. It didn't.

I met a lot of people over the course of three days in jail. A woman whose daughter was having a baby that week; she missed her first grandchild's birth. A father from Wisconsin who had just finished cramming a U-Haul's worth of his daughter's belongings into her tiny New York University dorm and had stepped out to get Chinese food. We all had simply been taken out of our lives.

After I begged hard, a cop slid his quarter-full water bottle through the bars to me. I asked the tall, soft-faced, middle-aged African American man, "Do you know that your civil rights were won by people who protested to gain them?"

"In just a few more years I get my pension," he said apologetically, turning away.

I thought back to the time after September 11. Letter-by-letter on the back of the fire barrels we'd made, Mikey and I had carved the initials NYPD to honor the New York City Police Department. We had etched, *Thank you for your service*. It seemed bizarre now, mixed up. But I knew that the fear I felt toward the police was not a fear of the *people* who wore the blue civil-servant costumes. I feared what commodified them.

Swap-O-Rama-Rama

That same year, in 2004, Americans were producing 13.1 million tons
of textile waste annually, according to the Environmental Protection
Agency. *Where is value in a commodified world?* I wondered. Before
becoming trash, the goods that fill the plastic bags that line the streets
were paid for with money that hardworking people earned. So why did
we immediately throw our hard work away?

Around that time, Larry Harvey, the founder of Burning Man,
gave a public talk at the Angel Orensanz Foundation for the Arts in
downtown Manhattan. He pointed out that a hundred years ago, when
people made more of their own goods, there was very little trash. He
reasoned that this was because handmade objects contain a different
kind of value: stories in the form of a memory, experience, a reminder
of a life lived. It is easy to notice that goods made by faceless computers
and industrial machines do not contain the kind of stories that people
treasure. And one might also ask of the manufactured thing: Was sweatshop labor used? Fossil fuels burned? Life-sustaining resources pillaged?
It is no wonder we throw them away. Perhaps the goods we make today
are being kicked to the curb because they remind us of our participation
in the diminishing of life.

It was time to use the skills I had reclaimed from the commodified
world to offer more than just a complaint.

 I will create a remedy for the lust for stuff.

TRANSFORM TRASH

We live amid the **LARGEST** surplus in the history of the world and most things can be found secondhand or in the trash. Reclaim the **CREATIVITY** that has been lost to industry. Make :VALUE: out of garbage.

DRESS MADE FROM CAUTION TAPE

GREENHOUSE FROM WATER BOTTLES

HOME STORAGE FROM BIKE BASKETS

I called my solution Swap-O-Rama-Rama. It's a clothing swap that makes use of the existing surplus of used clothing by creating new goods out of them. In DIY spirit and through workshops, creativity is reclaimed through the making of things. The barrier between consumer and creator is dissolved. Swap-O-Rama-Rama presents the hands-on discovery that the making of things is not an activity to be avoided in order to attain leisure, but a playful and leisurely endeavor unto itself.

After a successful first event in New York City and a grant from Burning Man's nonprofit Black Rock Arts, later that year at the first Maker Faire in California, thousands of people showed up for a west coast Swap-O-Rama-Rama. Glue guns, scissors, trim, patches, zippers, buttons, and board game pieces were passed back and forth by busy, inspired hands. With the swipe of squeegees, Trinity Cross's crew of silkscreen artists styled the old into the newly interesting. Andrea

At the 2006 Maker Faire Swap-O-Rama-Rama, textile artist Miranda Caroligne deconstructed and reconstructed an outfit as a live performance.

DeHart taught a workshop on how to transform socks into iPod covers; Stitch Lounge (a local sewing collective) offered a T-shirt reconstruction class; Sandy Drobny brought a loom with her to demonstrate her process for weaving plastic bags. She made colorful aprons adorned with thrift shop hair curlers. Emiko showed people how to transform old board-game pieces into jewelry. Ten local clothing designers armed with sewing machines taught people who had never sewed before how to transform used clothing into newish versions of things they imagined. Finally, by rebranding clothing with celebratory "Modified by Me" labels provided at the event, attendees were invited to see each other through shared creativity.

A few gems were placed in Swap-O-Rama-Rama's structure. Nothing would ever be for sale, all the materials to create with were free, and there would never be mirrors. This encouraged everyone to turn to one another to ask, "How do I look?" Immediate intimacy resulted. Friends made.

At a nearby table a guy from the botanical gardens was teaching a class on composting natural fibers like cotton and hemp using worms. In one arm he held a plastic tub with shredded paper and strips of cotton T-shirts pouring out of the top on all sides. Worms in sizes large to tiny slithered over the edges. A crew of ten-year-olds waited anxiously for a chance to touch the wiggling wonders of the earth. One asked if he could make something out of them.

Mikey explained radio frequency identification (RFID) to an attentive group. Then he demonstrated how to line old pants pockets with a metallic fiber fabric. Metallic fiber turns a regular pants pocket into a Faraday cage, blocking RFID readers from picking up personal information on credit cards and driver's licenses.

Since I had first experienced the gift economy in Black Rock City, I had searched for value everywhere in the default world. The heaps of trash lining city streets indicated where value was missing. Consumer goods did not contain it. At Swap-O-Rama-Rama, I saw value for the very first time. Workstations were crammed with people sewing by hand, by machine, by serger, producing textile wonders. Shoes were unstitched then refastened; grommets were pressed into leather, pleather, and plastic; flip-flops were zip-tied together into welcome mats; bras hacked into handbags; sweaters unknitted and reknitted. The random variety of zigzag stitches, odd-sized snaps, and peculiar patches of mismatched scraps made a stunning bazaar of irregularity. The garments, oddball, cockeyed, and strange, were imbued with meaning.

A career in marketing had taught me its aim: to divide people into categories based on lifestyle, habit, and socioeconomic status. When these categories become expressed as brands, people interpret themselves according to brand; they fit themselves and each other into lifestyle categories. In my own life I had been part Prana, part Apple, and even part Burning Man. Branding is an effective technique if you are a company selling products to consumers. But it teaches us to view other people through socioeconomic status and lifestyle before seeing each other as people. Brands say nothing of our creativity, our generosity, or the depth of our hearts; often they only represent how much money we have (or don't have).

At Swap-O-Rama-Rama people of all ages, ethnicities, cultures, and socioeconomic backgrounds gathered together; an unbranded identity broke through branding's categories, and people defined themselves by something different: their creativity.

After the first year, Swap-O-Rama-Rama grew to 25 cities, then to 125. Cities from Juneau, Alaska, to Huntsville, Alabama, to Waxahachie, Texas, and to places as far away as Istanbul, Jerusalem, Panama, Perth, and New Zealand have made it part of their way of life. I turned Swap-O-Rama-Rama into a nonprofit organization and collected donations from sponsors that I passed on to communities all over the world: sewing and silk-screening machines, scissors, fabric, and inks. I welcome all to join in and produce Swap-O-Rama-Rama for their communities. It's growing still.

Lukas silkscreened his own designs onto attendees' used duds and sent everyone away happy.

Can you believe this outfit was made out of old upholstery? Here it is at the 2006 Maker Faire Swap-O-Rama-Rama fashion show.

Nature Is the Truest Book

Nature loves to hide [Becoming is a secret process].
— HERACLITUS (TRANS. GUY DAVENPORT)

As a New Yorker I was well aware that my life was lived on top of a concrete shell that sealed the floor of a noisy metropolis. In Central Park, I celebrated 843 fortifying acres of lawn, garden, and frolicsome fountains. I knew where to find nooks to duck into for respite where silence could be imagined. The city contains niches for taking refuge made by people who know the value of the living. On the street I found nature persisting in window boxes and in 4-foot by 4-foot squares of soil breaking up the sidewalks, capturing stray litter, and providing a home to sturdy trees. As a city dweller, I was connected to the natural world only at the margins. The racket produced by commerce, dealing, traffic, merchandising, transactions, and negotiations was louder than the wind in the trees and the few birds that survived the concrete jungle.

I made occasional recovery trips to Jones Beach on Long Island and to Woodstock upstate. Free of the restriction of a full-time job, I enjoyed a luxurious three weeks in Central America, where I noticed that I had reached a deeper level of relaxation than any I'd known before. Something unwound. Just when I started to feel it, I was due to fly home. I earmarked the feeling of calm and noted that it came, given time, in the presence of the natural world.

When I was back in my Brooklyn apartment I dug out a book that had captured my attention years before. A scrap of paper still held the spot where the author, a Sufi, had written *Nature is the truest book*. The words seemed important to my pledges. A decommodified life must be related to nature. After all, if civilization itself were cleared from the earth, nature would remain.

I thought of Sufis as a secret tribe that existed half a world away, in desert caves or atop remote mountains, unnoticed by all but those who had to seek them out. I pictured myself, a Jewish girl from Long Island, trekking across a sunbaked, windy world in search of them. *Some must,* I thought, wondering if I was one who must. Just those few words, *Nature is the truest book*, had inspired years of my gathering and reading Sufi books. The writings of Sufis throughout history have offered remedies for the impulses that drive materialism. Often they allude to a magic toolbox linked to nature. Embedded in a rich lineage of love poetry, a trail of clues points to a domain beyond the lust for stuff, a vibrant and abundant world waiting to be found. I spent my twenties and part of my thirties poring over the Sufis' carefully woven words and trying to decipher their paradoxical and encrypted language.

I decided that if I acted like a Sufi, if I did what Sufis do, I might find out more about them. So, as though it were some kind of game, I did what I thought a Sufi might do. The Sufis are known for wearing whatever cloak is necessary for the task at hand, and so I changed the way I looked and acted, to see what I would learn. "I wonder what shy people experience?" I queried. I practiced being meek and went out into the world in the guise of a bashful person. People who had never before noticed me found me approachable. They were scientific types and other shy people with personalities too refined to have approached the animated personality that I now hid away. Life opened up; my perspective widened. When I felt boredom, I switched it for an itch on my foot. I changed anxiety to curiosity. Each experiment led me into worlds that had always been there but I had not noticed.

These games prompted me to consider that the most ordinary aspects of life could be awe-inspiring. Magic was buried in the obvious and plainly evident but not noticed. To apply this new view to the world around me, I made time to notice the veins in the leaves that fell to the ground, studied the sound of the wind with marked interest, and savored the scent of whatever the breeze carried my way. I was stunned to realize how much I had missed the richness that permeates life. I included people as part of nature and met each face as a representative of the natural world. The shared thoughts and feelings of others became treasures.

After many months of playing Sufi I determined that it was time to seek out the mysterious dervishes whose secret keys to nature would surely help me to discover a decommodified life.

In a small community garden near my Brooklyn apartment, under a giant tree that canopied the lot and the two that neighbored it, I opened my laptop and punched the words *Sufi New York* into a search engine. The first thing to pop up was a four-year study in Sufi philosophy. It was laid out in 10-day increments two times a year. It was set to begin in two weeks. Without hesitating, I enrolled.

Twelve days later I was surrounded by old forest and lush medicinal gardens, at a former Shaker village upstate, a couple hours' drive from Manhattan. I was with the Sufis. I had absolutely no idea what to expect of the adventure about to begin, but I did know that I was where I was meant to be.

As surely as we inhabit the environment, the environment inhabits us.

— Pir Zia Inayat-Khan

I kept the rubber breathing tube clutched firmly between my front teeth. I probed it with my tongue to make sure that a small movement would not separate me from it. *What if a bug above ground crawls in? I'll have to blow it out. . . or eat the critter.*

ABUNDANCE

I didn't know if I could get out of my earthen grave. The weight of the earth above my naked body prevented me from taking a full breath. When I inhaled, the earth pushed back on my lungs, informing me of my limited capacity. I took small sips of air and imagined the winter woods above as the cold came through the narrow plastic tube. In thirty minutes my partner, Isfandarmudh ("angel of the earth" in Persian), would dig me out of the grave. Then I would bury her.

I turned my attention away from the fear of things that could go wrong. I relaxed my active mind with a long, slow exhale, imagining my skin fading into the earth that pressed against it.

My bones, teeth, and nails conversed with the minerals in the stones and tectonic plates of the earth. The heat in my body reached out to find the molten core of the underworld. I wondered if the bugs that crawled behind one of my ears, under my arm, around the top of a fingertip, and all along my body were taking in moisture from the thin layer of perspiration on my surface. I felt something behind my knee.

I am made mostly of water, I thought as I considered the geothermal waters that filled veins in the earth and made up most of my body, the rain that poured from dark cumulonimbus clouds and saturated the ground from which I myself drank. *There is one water on earth,* I reminded myself.

From head to toe I felt life wiggle and walk. *Don't panic, Jehanara.* This was my new Sufi name. *This is what it feels like to host life.* Giving up fear to the forces of gravity and the magnetic fields that banded the planet, I knew that I could never overwhelm the massive systems with my worry. I felt no different from a tangled root or a wedge of clay. The grave smelled like mildew and growth.

It was good to *be* the earth. I reviewed a long history: a singularity split in two, gaseous explosions, a hot lava-covered sphere of volcanic eruptions and shifting plates, a cooler water world, a single cell advancing to more complex organisms, fish, bird, mammal. I was curious. *What next?*

Life's lust is life, I thought as I considered that life's persistence over billions of years has led to me. I felt obliged to use my senses so that this life could know itself.

The feeling of earth that pressed against me from every direction changed my view. I imagined it as a hug. *You are loved.* That's what the Sufi teachers said to do if I ever forgot that I was loved: *Feel the tug of gravity.* In this moment death did not feel definitive. My sense of self expanded to include all time. I remembered the words that I had read in that little book written by a Sufi. *Nature is the truest book.*

The sound of a metal shovel breaking through the ground above me brought me back. *I hope she doesn't hit me with that!*

During my first year with the Sufis I learned that it is their habit to visit the outposts of the senses and by doing so extend the edge of the map that marks life's reach. I had come to the Sufis to obtain the magic keys to access nature. What I learned from them is that *we* are those keys.

I will advance from skills useful in a world made by human beings to those essential for life.

Ladybugs in New York City

To know that we know what we know, and that we do not know
what we do not know, that is true knowledge.

— Confucius

On the drive home from the Sufis, thick vines creeping along hardly visible fences spoke out to me as though distant relatives. Lush green meadows wooed me to stop the car and stroll. But sweet single-lane country roads eventually led me downstate and to the four lanes of highway required to handle the volume of activity that buzzed just north of the city. Then I was back in New York City's traffic, but without the impulse to rush along with it. I was following different opportunities now, taking my time and noticing the life of this world.

When I got back to our apartment, I found a package waiting in my mailbox. *Open immediately* was scrawled in black marker. I excitedly broke the tape seal with scissors, and then, holding the box out an open window, I shook it over the tomato plant that sat on my fourth-story fire escape. Out came the 2,500 ladybugs that I'd ordered on the Internet. At that moment, traffic on the Williamsburg Bridge above caused a familiar tremor and tiny lead-paint chips sprinkled down, covering me, the plant, and the ladybugs. It was a holocaust. The red-and-black nonpareils rained down into the foot-wide gap between my building and the one next to it. I thought about how odd this would seem to the people in the apartments below.

Twenty-five hundred ladybugs was the minimum order. Until that very moment, I hadn't considered that they would need food. I had read that tomato plants need pollinators in order to bear fruit. The plants on my fire escape grew tall and green but remained fruitless. I didn't realize that ladybugs were a poor choice for pollination. And I didn't order aphids to feed the ladybugs, though if someone had told me that it would help, I probably would have done that, too. I didn't have a whole lot of common sense about the natural world. It's probably a good thing that the tomato plant never produced a fruit — if it had, I may have eaten it and dropped dead.

That was my first attempt at growing food. The intelligence that I had to throw at the problem was the kind that people gather growing up in cities and suburbs. I had plenty of the kind of savvy that helped me travel on public transportation, use a cash machine, or find a good Chinese restaurant. But not the kind of knowledge that helps one read the sky for signs of shifting weather, start a fire without a match, or grow plants. The ladybug experience was frustrating, but I recognized from it that I had a desire for another kind of knowledge.

I told Mikey about the name given to me by the Sufis.

"Jehanara — it means queen of the universe!" I said. "Not civilization's universe, that's called *dunya* (the Arabic word for the false world glommed on top of the real). I'm queen of *jehan*, the real world that is everlasting."

A Sufi name indicates something that a person is meant to achieve, her purpose. I thought about the pledges I had made and treasured the meaning of my new name.

What Is the Cost of a Job?

Those who want to master the future must create it.
— TRADITIONAL SAYING

The next day Mikey and I took the subway deeper into Brooklyn to look at an apartment for sale. When we got off the train we walked a block farther into a neighborhood that New Yorkers call transitional. Which means that it probably had a high crime rate and a good deal of poverty, but young white people were moving in and things were soon to "turn around." That's what people always said when neighborhoods gentrified. I wondered if New York City was going to go the way of Paris, where the poor people who had been pushed out of the city moved into once-wealthy suburbs that themselves turned into slums. *Poor people have to go somewhere,* I thought. In the years I had lived in the city, I had seen people in "transitional" neighborhoods lose their homes and culture as people with more financial resources moved in.

Ron, the building manager, pulled up in his new-model Volvo. We climbed through the dangerously unfinished building and walked on planks that bridged a three-story-high gap in the floor. "$750,000," he said, though we had not asked. "Taxes are probably going to be around $6,000, maybe $10,000, maybe $12,000, hard to say. For an extra $50,000 cash, I can throw in a parking space." I saw a clear and distinct image of Mikey and me wearing matching metal shackles attached to long chains, tied to desks inside the cubicles that fill the city's skyscrapers. I turned to Mikey and said, "Let's go." We both knew that I meant, "Let's get out of New York."

The next morning Mikey headed out the door to work in a navy blue jumpsuit with a zipper up the front and an embroidered white Con Edison logo on the large breast pocket.

"Where are you going in that?" I asked. He worked for a bank!

"I'm quitting," he said, and winked.

He wore a Chuck E. Cheese uniform the next day. The higher-ups in his department interpreted his odd behavior as proof of his brilliance — eccentric geeks are expected in the world of information technology — and they gave him a handsome raise.

At home that evening, armed with a sewing machine and a soldering iron, he set to work replacing each pinstripe of a Brooks Brothers suit with strands of illuminated wire. He rigged the contraption to a homemade circuit board and set it to blink a variety of lively patterns. The one time Band-Aid Boy put on the wearable gizmo and went out into the evening, a spectacle and a silent protest.

Mikey had been working in a cubicle at a Wall Street bank for nine years. Like the wife of a doctor on call, I was used to him running off into the night. Not to save a person's life, but to protect the banking giant from technical vulnerability. The stock market must never stop and must never, ever be vulnerable. It's no fun knowing that the fruit of your labor is being used to no-good ends, and Mikey winced each time his employer applied for a patent in his name. An open-source programmer, Mikey imagined a world in which knowledge belonged to anyone who needed it and not just to wealthy banks using it to sharpen their competitive edge. Both he and I wished to contribute to the commons rather than the forces that prop up a world whose priority is money.

It was late 2005 and Mikey had just completed the several-year project of shifting the giant bank to a Linux operating system, an open-source system that connected the bankers to the world of what is shared. Mikey announced that it was time to make our move.

We knew that leaving the city meant detaching from reliable income and the only lifestyle we knew, so we rolled out a whiteboard and grabbed our erasable markers to take inventory of the expenses of life. We noted, in particular, how many expenses related to having a job. We asked a fundamental question that had never before occurred to us.

WHAT IS THE COST OF A JOB?

EXPENSIVE CLOTHING	LAUNDERING of that clothing	THE NEED TO LIVE IN OR NEAR CITIES where the cost of living is high
COMMUTING (fuel/public transportation)	MEALS EATEN OUT	SLEEP LOST, HEALTH DIMINISHED BY STRESS
TIME that could be spent making replaced with money to spend buying	NO TIME TO LEARN TO BE INDEPENDENT	REWARDS TO OURSELVES FOR WHAT WE'VE GIVEN UP (vacations, expensive consumer goods)

The list we made revealed that many of life's expenses could be avoided altogether by just getting rid of the job.

For the first time since I had quit my job and set out in my Honda, I felt that I had everything I needed to do just about anything. I had reclaimed my skills, found Mikey, discovered yoga — something I could barter or gift — and was learning the Sufis' keys to nature.

When Mikey announced that he was leaving, the manager of his department at the Wall Street bank said, "I don't know how to process this — no one ever quits."

The sky Is the ocean

Amidst chaos there is harmony. . . . He who is prepared to listen
to it will catch the tone.

— SWAMI VIVEKANANDA

A few months later we began to visit places where we might want to
live. We traveled to Panama, where by a week's end the host, jani-
tor, landscaper, cook, and driver for our hotel, a guy named Eduardo,
relieved us of a kitten we had plucked from a sewer drain and nursed
with an eyedropper. In Panama, cats were of equal value to rats, but our
host amused us with politeness. He took Pipito by the scruff of his neck
with two fingers and, wearing a strained smile, assured us our surrogate
pet would go to a farm and become a well-employed mouse catcher. We
cat lovers didn't fit in Panama. Besides, to live there, we quickly saw
we would have to choose between being rich and being poor. The rich
had nice homes and armed guards. The poor had interesting handmade
shacks and indigenous skills. No one had a pet cat.

We visited northern California, but realized that city and suburban life there felt too much like the lifestyle we already knew well. We
were seeking the unfamiliar — a way of life that offered the greatest
possible growth.

I had once visited New Mexico, a.k.a. the Land of Enchantment, to
attend the spring wedding of friends who had left New York to move
there. New Mexico greeted Mikey and me with the same white-yellow
light that had drenched the skies on that trip. We'd left behind a gray
winter in New York.

"Imagine not getting seasonal light depression every year," I whispered to Mikey.

While waiting for a bus, I asked a man who told us he'd lived in the desert for 30 years if he missed the ocean. "The sky is the ocean," he replied, looking up to receive a face full of white light from the blue dome above. The bright sun cast a movie-set sheen on his brown weathered face.

We drove a long way south across what seemed a barren, monochromatic landscape of beige and brown before arriving in a small town called Truth or Consequences. We met up with the couple whose wedding I had attended and then spent Thanksgiving going from house to house nibbling turkey and sipping wine. The town's newest round of residents, mostly couples in their thirties and forties and young retirees, were eager to meet us. They were new to T or C, as they called it, and to small-town life. They had come from places like Los Angeles, New Jersey, New York, Montana, Michigan, and Minnesota to search out a simpler way of life. Many had recently become the town's small business owners. They ran coffee shops, clothing stores, consignment shops, art galleries, and hotels. A woman from Glen Cove, a town I'd once lived in on Long Island, ran a cozy bookstore called the Black Cat. *Pioneers!* I thought, flashing a look of excitement at Mikey.

In a coffee shop that seconded as an art gallery and felt a lot like a movie set done up in a western theme, I observed several gay cowboys come and go, each wearing a tall hat, pointy boots, and a fancy belt buckle. After an exchange of small talk with everyone in the place, each went out the door, back into the illuminated desert world. We watched the flow of customers. A team of paramedics took their caffeine to go. Everyone was enthusiastic about life in T or C, which was all they talked about. The stores along Main Street and Broadway featured non-specific signs that indicated strange business hours, OPEN 11ISH TO 4ISH and I'M SORRY TO SAY WE'RE OPEN. The town featured 25 art galleries, almost one for every church.

The rest of the community of under 10,000 people, I was told, was made up of poorer folks, families who had lived in the area for several generations, ranchers, people let out of mental hospitals when the state stopped funding them, war veterans, and the standard fare of American meth addicts. A 30-something Italian woman from New Jersey referred to them as Methopotamians. Later I would learn that southwestern desert towns are hideouts for people who don't want to be found. Thirty miles from T or C, Virgin Galactic was preparing to begin construction of a spaceport to offer the first consumer flights to the lower atmosphere. Eventually, the town grew to include a Buddhist stupa (shrine), which seemed to me a metaphorical cherry on top of an alien-themed Carvel cake.

In late 2006, Truth or Consequences was booming. But the town's growth was not the kind that Mikey and I had witnessed in New York, when each year we were forced to move to a rattier neighborhood with more muggings in order to make room for Starbucks, unaffordable gourmet groceries, and higher rents. It didn't seem that the small desert town was going to fall victim to the kind of fast-paced gentrification that wipes out preexisting ethnic communities and then later

The Sky Is the Ocean

WHAT'S IN A PLACE?
TRUTH OR CONSEQUENCES, NEW MEXICO

LOW COST OF LIVING: inexpensive property, taxes, and goods	**A DEBT-FREE LIFE:** work less, live more	**HOT SPRINGS:** mineral spring aquifer and a relaxed culture of people who like to soak	**SUNSHINE:** no more light depression
LOW POPULATION DENSITY	**CLEAN AIR**	**WATER:** many aquifers, two lakes	**ABUNDANT NATURAL RESOURCES:** hundreds of miles of desert in almost every direction
260+ DAY GROWING SEASON: better food for less money	**WARM CLIMATE = LOWER UTILITY USE:** opportunity for solar hot water and power, lower heating needs	**A NEWLY EMERGING COMMUNITY**	**MODERN PIONEERING**
FLEXIBLE BUILDING CODES	**A PROGRESSIVE COMMUNITY:** welcoming and friendly, creative people	**A HEALTHY LIFESTYLE:** hiking, exploring, nature	**A DECOMMODIFIED LIFESTYLE**
A CULTURE OF PEOPLE WHO MAKE THINGS, ACQUISITION OF NEW SKILLS	**CULTURE SHOCK = PERSONAL GROWTH**	**HIGH-SPEED INTERNET**	**DAILY MAIL DELIVERY AND PICKUP:** USPS, FedEx, UPS

makes tourism out of their culture — though this had indeed been the fate of the Apache Indians who had lived in the area decades before. A few doors down from the coffee shop, a local museum chronicled Geronimo's fight to save a dying way of life. Talk in town was that an Apache curse had been laid on the land by Geronimo's people. The curse had an expiration date of 2004. That was just about the time all the people we met had started moving in. New Mexicans like stories and have the time to tell them. They especially favor those about New Mexico, Native Americans, and space aliens.

T or C was growing slowly, one property at a time. No two buildings were alike, each a peculiar harmonizing of unmatched parts made to fit together in spite of being the remnants of dozens of other projects. The whole place seemed to have been constructed piecemeal from what could be plucked from dumpsters. Tacked-together scraps made quirky fences, unusual ceilings, and sturdy sheds that all said in no uncertain terms that this place was not commodified. T or C is part Mad Max and part Burning Man, with remnants of the Wild West strung together in avant-garde fashion and tethered to third world simplicity.

That night, in a hot tub next to the Rio Grande, under a star-studded sky, we asked each other, "What will we do here?" T or C was a place that invited us to dream aloud. We were content with the only answer available at the time: "We'll figure it out."

part II

LIFE
HANDS-ON

Makers of shelter

Many think that life is not interesting because they make
nothing, but they do not realize that they have to make a world,
that they are making a world, either ignorantly or wisely. If they
make a world ignorantly then that world is their captivity; if they
make a world wisely then that world is their paradise.

— HAZRAT INAYAT KHAN

"Warm up by the fire before it goes out," said a voice from the darkness as I stood and turned toward the Airstream to hit the sack. I took a single swig of the homemade hooch being passed around that night and stood with my back to the fire. The brew was awful, but the patch of heat in my middle was worth it.

I followed a moonlit trail to the 10-foot by 5-foot trailer, balanced on cinderblocks, that served as storage shed and guest house. I expected it to give way when I climbed aboard and added my weight in between the rows of boxes.

"Maybe it'll help me pass out, so I won't know how uncomfortable I am," I whispered to Mikey.

"Voices carry," he reminded sternly.

The yipping sound of a coyote pack informed us of a kill scored nearby, a bunny, maybe a small javelina. It was cold this New Year's Eve.

"I can't believe they bought forty acres for less than $10,000 *and* they don't pay taxes," I whispered.

The trendy young couple putting us up had one bill to pay. It was for a phone that they shared between them. They were *free*.

Property in the land grant in Terlingua, Texas, came with very low taxes. Sure, there were a few thorns, things that had to be lived with.

I'm not even talking about the goathead thorns, vicious little spiked barbs that pierce through boots like rattlesnake fangs. Regional dogs hop three-legged waiting for sympathetic humans to pluck the free-loader seed from their calloused paws. I'm talking about the absence of conveniences that most of us take for granted: running water, paved roads, and an electric grid. In scorching heat, people who own property erect metal roofs and giant empty cisterns. After seasonal rains fill the cisterns, the landowners return, park a trailer, and try to survive the desert while they build a permanent home. Every building supply is an hour's drive and gallons of fuel away. Some who attempt to live in Terlingua fail because it is too hot for labor most hours of the day, most days of the year. There is no shade unless you build it, and there are many reasons to take siestas.

Some build forever. With no overhead there is little need for a job and no rush to finish anything. This suits those who build out of scrap just fine. Finding good junk requires patience. You've got to be in the right spot at the right moment. Jobs interfere with the melody of seren-dipity required for getting the best scores.

The homestead where we spent New Year's Eve is part of a low-tax land grant in Terlingua, Texas.

Makers of Shelter

The earth-cracked town of Terlingua sits just north of the Mexican border, buffered by Big Bend National Park. In the center of town, a long, creaky wooden porch greets guests before they find three doors: the roadhouse bar Star Light, a gift shop, and a bookstore. Rockers with their backs to the brutal western sun sit next to ashtrays spilling over with cigarette butts, facing a view of a dusty cemetery filled with makeshift tombstones. Mexican candles, light-scorched photos, and sun-bleached plastic flowers mark the graves.

Mikey and I were in Terlingua to meet builders who work with papercrete, a fibrous material made of reused paper. A few people in the region were rumored to be building houses with it. Everyone chose papercrete for the same reasons: it is an easy-to-work-with waste material that can be obtained free, and it offers significant insulation. Back in Truth or Consequences, Mikey and I had just spent the better part of a year experimenting with it. We had been making papercrete blocks at the rate of 200 a day. The blocks filled our property, making it look as though a cemetery full of tombstones had sprung up overnight. The road trip was a needed break from labor, an effort to satisfy our curiosity about what other builders had been making with the stuff, and an excuse to tour the region that was our new home, the southwestern United States.

Before leaving our hosts, we took a good look at their desert setup. It was tidy and reflected good planning. I had the impression that the couple was newly married and that wedding money had bought everything in sight. Four cisterns that held a combined 10,000 gallons of water sat along the end of a thermal-resistant roof that shaded their stylish vintage Airstream. Along the trailer's south side, rows of potted plants, mostly vegetables and herbs and a few rare-variety cacti, sat between the trailer and a huge screen of dark shade cloth that was pulled taut and resisted wind. The screen, an impressive 20 feet by 10 feet, softened the sun's brassy ultraviolet rays, giving the plants a chance to thrive. In the desert a garden's success relies on time out of the sun.

Beyond the screen, two outdoor picnic tables baking in the heat made the dining room. A few feet farther, an antique porcelain clawfoot tub sat atop a handmade platform. A modest photovoltaic (PV) solar setup with four batteries had been carefully positioned in the path of the sun.

They have everything they need, I thought. I wondered if I could live so close to the bone.

The couple who had built the next homestead we visited had left Terlingua because it was becoming "too developed." A $50 annual fee to service a paved road had pushed them to wilder territory on the other side of the border. They were building a new homestead in Mexico. Abe and Josie knew that a $50 annual fee could lead to other fees and eventually the need for a job.

We spent the day tooling around the lot they had left behind, discussing what could be revealed about the techniques they used to build their mud slipform structure. We found a pile of fans that we figured were collected for their motors. Abe built small wind turbines out of trash. By now I was used to visiting people's junk piles. I thought of them the way that I had once thought of the free boxes on the steps

Abe and Josie left behind their slip-form mud home and headed to Mexico to avoid a $50 road fee and possible future expenses.

Makers of Shelter

of Brooklyn brownstones. But junk piles are not always free. In the Southwest, junk plays an important part in the local domestic economy. It has value. If you find yourself perusing a junk pile, you're probably being offered a gift.

Behind the house, we found an outbuilding that housed a battery bank, the repository for the power generated by a PV solar and turbine setup that was still functioning when we arrived. An elegant black widow spider hung down in front of the only door to the power room, as though guarding the loot. Having lived in the desert for over a year, we were accustomed to negotiating with the impressive venomous creatures. We rolled newspaper into a tube shape and set it on fire, whispered an apology to the life of this world, admired for a moment the lovely lady's fine architectural lines, and torched her.

"When you are this far from a hospital you can't take chances," we reasoned. With the bounty unguarded, we were able to connect a few detached wires and get power running in the house.

A pair of rusty Frigidaire doors from the 1950s opened like an entryway to a western saloon and gave us access to a garden inside a fence made out of dozens of 4-foot-long stalks from the ocotillo plant. The thorn-covered posts had been stabbed into the ground 3 feet apart. They were strung together with barbed wire, making a low-cost barrier to keep out critters. A few heads of lettuce and tomato plants persisted in the soil.

"It must have rained recently," Mikey said, fingering the lettuce as though considering it for dinner.

Cisterns around the place were full of rainwater. One could easily move in and begin to live in the still-working homestead.

The slipform mud home was designed for thermal gain. A sturdy building, it suffered only from being absent of life. Dust blew through windows that had shaken loose from their hinges. We spent the night on the floor in the loft perched high above an open living room. For warmth, we lit a fire in the tiny handmade clay potbelly stove below.

These rusty fridge doors from the 1950s lead to a garden.

Abe and Josie's handmade fireplace features their baby's handprints and has a BBQ lid for a door.

The chimney, molded by hand, resembled a tall tree with lumpy bark and gnarled limbs. A small set of handprints indicated that their first child had participated in the making of it. The stove's door was made from the top of a rusted barbecue set on a hinge.

On the earthen stove we heated the tamales we'd made at home. We had carried them in a cooler so that we did not have to rely on restaurants while on the road. After filling up on black bean and cheese tamales, we prepared for the darkness that was already creeping in.

The next day we visited a property that was rumored to have a papercrete structure. The compound was a sprawl of rusted-out vehicles, half-finished domes, and dusty trailers. A rowdy herd of goats and a not-so-friendly dog guarded the loot. With trepidation we toured the compound, finding interesting-looking homemade jigs for bending the rebar that made up the armature of a well insulated papercrete dome. The dome provided shelter for the bearded goats. The dog favored a patch of shade produced by a mesquite tree. We never found the owner.

In Marathon, Texas, housing conditions improved when we arrived at Eve's Garden, a papercrete hotel hand-built by Clyde Curry. Clyde set us up with a purple, red, and metallic gold room decorated in pretty textiles. It had an impressive domed ceiling and a soft, comfy bed. After settling in, we joined our host in his library. We sat before a warm fire and thumbed through Clyde's collection of building books. We talked about the heroes of our craft: Clyde, about Nader Khalili and a guy in Mexico who started a website and built a compound called Flying Concrete; and Mikey, about French builder Antti Lovag and his protégé Robert Bruno. I like Middle Eastern architecture, Moroccan and other African structures made by no one in particular, community efforts using skills passed down for so long that they became innate. My favorite building book is Christopher Alexander's *Pattern Language*.

Clyde Curry built Eve's Garden, a papercrete hotel, in Marathon, Texas.

That night we drank wine and savored delicious food grown in an indoor greenhouse that connected one part of the large hotel to another. Its humidity helped hold the building's heat. In spite of outside temperatures in the teens, the hotel did not require artificial heating. We discussed tensile strength, R-value (a measure of insulation efficiency), solar gain, square footage (circumference and area), dry times, and cost per square foot, and when we could no longer keep our eyes open, we took a quick dip in the indoor lap pool and went off to sleep in our majestic papercrete room.

Lying on the bed that night and noticing the accumulation of moisture that Mikey's shower had produced on the domed papercrete ceiling, I wondered if the condensation was cause for worry. Paper can mold if not well sealed. But the heavy latex paint that Clyde had applied thickly and everywhere seemed more than adequate.

I felt like a total pansy on much of the trip. My good-looking but wimpy street shoes had made hiking treacherous. I didn't think to pack a flashlight or enough warm clothes, and I had no idea which plants were to be avoided and which were to be eaten in a pinch. Our Terlingua hosts had sprung from their trailer each morning looking perky, clean, and well dressed, while I flopped out of our shed dirty and disoriented, making futile efforts to wash my face with what seemed like an eyedropper of precious water.

A year of building in the desert had made me capable of having sophisticated conversations about building with people like Clyde, and yet a door that divided the cozy life of Eve's Garden from the unforgiving desert was all that prevented me from being as useless as a sapphire cocktail ring. In the desert I felt as though I were on a ship stranded at sea and didn't know how to swim. I had learned about building shelter, but I still didn't know how to survive in the world outside of it.

Cooking and sleeping outdoors, knowing how to find drinkable water, and reading upcoming weather conditions by looking at the sky were not skills I had yet. More than 30 years of acculturated knowledge made me perfectly able to operate a bidet, avoid paying retail, and get a free parking spot almost anywhere in New York City. But I could not conceive that a 50-degree change in temperature was possible in the same day, nor was I prepared for it when it happened.

I remembered the stories told days before by the sturdy desert dwellers who sat around the fire. There was one about living in the back of a pickup truck with a dog for 10 years, working a stint counting trees while residing in a tent deep in a forest for several months, and serving as a firewatcher in an 8-foot by 8-foot cabin miles from the nearest road. My contribution to the conversation sounded something like, "Put me in any New York City neighborhood any time of night and I am not scared." I had no idea that city folks are notorious for saying these kinds of things (lest their value go unrecognized by those who wield a different variety of knowledge). Desert dwellers knew such things as after becoming dehydrated out in the desert, the first sip of water should be used to wash the toxins out of your mouth and spit on the ground. And there's what to do if a forest fire broke out and there was no time to run from it. You could jump into a water tank. If the fire passed over fast and you got out before the water boiled, you might survive. I was not a New Mexican yet. I did not have a dog of the heeler variety or a nonworking toilet serving as art in my yard, although both were soon to come.

With my ego stuffed deep in my pocket, below the pack of hand-wipes that it became my habit to carry in case I was offered another hole in the ground to poop in, I thought about the image I had crafted of myself as the outdoorsy type and reviewed where this impression came from. In day camp, my group twice won the best campsite award because of a fence, a fire pit, and a swing that I designed. As a little girl, I had imagined tending a garden and filling an odd lot of dusty bottles with exotic plant remedies. I built sturdy forts in the woods behind my house. At Burning Man I made an impressive outdoor shower that everyone wanted to use. Many people who knew me thought I was really tough. But I'd been hanging out in French restaurants too long. I definitely couldn't light a fire without a match. The only plant I had ever grown was fruitless and died on my fire escape back in Brooklyn.

This is what I came for, I thought to myself. *To find the edge, the point at which my knowledge ends.* I was exactly where I want to be: uncomfortable. What I was itching for was something new. It was *common sense.* I didn't mind feeling ill at ease as long I was getting nearer to it. I considered the ways to acquire common sense: by living close to nature, by playing, by making mistakes, by taking time for contemplation, by allowing for trial and error, by listening, by building, by problem-solving, by maintaining relationships, by hiking, by growing plants, by cooking. Really, I didn't know. But I suspected that it would come from experience and not just from reading books or hearing of it being told.

Mikey and I toured more of the southwestern United States, stopping at alternative-building hot spots: Alpine, Texas; Tucson, Arizona; Crestone, Colorado; and Questa and Taos in northern New Mexico, to name a few. We surveyed unusual buildings made of straw bales, rastra, papercrete, earth-block, and ferro-cement; tallied the attributes of each material used; and noted their flaws and benefits. We inspected rounded earth ships that seemed to have evolved in the landscape naturally and along with the boulders jutting up next to them. We sat in simple teepees, Quonset huts, homey yurts, and kiva domes, and when we were lucky, we met their quirky and inspired makers. Though the people we met lived lives different from anything we'd experienced, and came from backgrounds nothing like ours, our common ground was immediately evident. We were working on essential problems: shelter, fuel, food, water, and power. We sought a life free of drudgework and a way to live in balance with nature. I thought of Swap-O-Rama-Rama and the way that it brought together people of all ages, colors, and socioeconomic statuses. In the desert, creativity connected people to life and to each other, too.

building in Truth or Consequences

Build like you give a damn.
— Mike Warren

Back in T or C, we were nearly finished remodeling a 40-year-old mobile home, the only building on the ratty 1-acre RV park that we had purchased just after we arrived in New Mexico. We had never intended to run or manage an RV park. Our plan was to build an off-grid bed and breakfast entirely by hand and out of waste materials. We chose an RV park as the site for the project because of the value of its infrastructure: power, water, sewer, and electric spaced every 20 feet. Though meant to accommodate trailers that plug in for short stays, the same infrastructure was perfect for plugging in our new handmade papercrete buildings. That's what we planned. We imagined that the preexisting infrastructure would save us a fortune in plumbing and electric, that one day a PV solar array would send clean solar power to each post, that a humanure setup would make sewer connections dispensable, and that cisterns would replace our need for city water. Our RV park also came with flexible zoning that allowed for a village of papercrete bungalows.

The mobile home needed a lot of work before we could call it home. The decrepit, ancient land ship still bearing a yellow New Mexico license plate had been manufactured in 1967. Over the years, several cheap extensions had been added on, expanding it to about

1,200 square feet. Our insurance company valued the jalopy at $1,000. This made it easy for us to make the greenest choice. We remodeled it.

The decision to remodel came easy. We were given a quote of $5,000 to haul the old mobile home to the landfill, and we compared that to the estimated cost of $10,000 to remodel it. With new construction costing no less than $200 per square foot, we ruled that out as an option. Since neither of us came to New Mexico with building experience, we figured we'd cut our teeth on the mobile. "If we destroy it, who cares?" we said to each other. We did not have much to lose.

The renovation consisted of covering paneled walls with new drywall, installing bamboo floors where there had been shag carpet, and laying a new floor in the bathroom that we made from broken throwaway tile found in the trash. We trimmed the windows, doorways, and floorboards with wood plucked from the garbage and resurfaced with a planer obtained at a garage sale. In each east-facing window, we added shelves to hold seedlings getting a start on life before going out to the garden we were soon to build. We added inexpensive bullnoses from the hardware store to round out square corners and made the space feel soft, clean, and modern.

Much of the wood came from projects so ancient that below a dirty surface we discovered handsome hardwoods with marbled patterns. Had we tried to purchase them new, they would have been not only too expensive, but also inappropriate considering their scarcity.

Since the appliances, cabinets, and basins were all functional, we kept them, scrubbing them clean and rubbing those made of wood with linseed oil to enliven their appearance and extend their life. Inexpensive aluminum flashing made a tough waterproof kitchen back wall and concealed dirty, sagging fiberboard beneath. The flashing filled the space between the kitchen counters and the cabinets; shiny and silver in color, it made our kitchen look like a 1950s diner. An even row of self-tapping screws of the same silver finish made the choice of industrial materials seem intentional.

The cost of the remodel did come in around $10,000 — approximately $10 a square foot. The first and best thing about it was that we gained a lovely home — and almost every bit of it was waste that had been saved from going to a landfill. The second best thing was that we acquired skills by doing it. Skills that might have cost thousands of dollars had we acquired them by attending a trade school.

We did not go it alone. Mikey and I found Jesse the scrap builder remodeling an old house in our neighborhood. Each day, Jesse hauled garbage from one side of the street to the other. Where a neighbor was tearing down an old outbuilding and piling the wood from it by a dumpster, Jesse saw opportunity and repurposed every scrap. He reworked the wood into cabinets, trim, and counters for his client's kitchen. One by one he ran the ratty old planks through an unbalanced planer on a makeshift table. When the planks came out the other side of the device, pretty patterns of contrasting light and dark colors appeared. Effortlessly he applied a coat of sealant while smiling in deserved self-appreciation. The wood seemed to smile back at him. We hired Jesse right away and became his apprentices. Together the three of us remodeled our mobile home in three months' time.

In some ways Jesse is a typical New Mexican. We learned that it was best not to expect him to come to work if the clouds covered the sun. The absence of light was something that made him feel too sentimental to cope. To employ Jesse, we first had to find him a place to live, a protocol common in the nomadic Southwest. A borrowed trailer sufficed for a temporary home for our roving builder. He parked it on our lot, next to the city bus that he'd converted into a workshop.

Once Jesse finished any part of a job, he had to be removed from the place before he could destroy it. Though he was gifted with the ability to transform waste into beauty, he also bore the curse of clumsiness. He once gave me a tour of a finished room of freshly sheetrocked walls while digging a groove in the wall with the tip of a sharp metal T-square that jutted out from the tool belt hanging from his waist.

By the end of the remodel, Mikey and I had acquired enough skills to work on our own. We learned the names of the tools and materials and how to use them: a chop saw for cutting lengths of trim and flooring, a table saw to thin woods to needed sizes, a finish gun to mount trim, a floor stapler to install wood flooring, trowels and hawks to cover sheetrock seams with plaster (after taping the joints with fiberglass tape), a diamond saw for tile cutting, a sander and a planer for bringing out new surfaces of woods, a variety of drills and an assortment of attachments, a jigsaw for cutting wood into free-form shapes, and a variety of solvents and oils for reviving and sealing wood and other materials.

We planned and then built garden beds, irrigation systems, and distillers. We made shade structures and everything from skateboards for moving heavy things to fences, sheds, and fire pits. I hurdled over and over again past a preset "I can't do that" by doing it anyway. We made mistakes and built things that could have been better but were good enough. I invested myself in the doing and avoided being caught up in expectations that might prevent me from taking a next step. Sometimes this was very difficult. At times Mikey and I argued over design and method because I could not reconcile with the idea of making something imperfect. Old habits are hard to break. Having a spirit of reckless experimentation was necessary.

In the desert Mikey discovered that knowledge he had carried around for much of his life and only occasionally found uses for — things like melting points, measurements of distances, conversion tables, flammability of gases, friction and leverage, weight limits, boiling points, and elevation — was invaluable when applied to the new lives we were living as makers of things. I filled sketchbooks with colorful drawings of domes, hot tubs, and gardens. From the moment we touched down in New Mexico we were enlivened by the challenge to create a 1-acre wonder world. First we imagined, and then we built what we saw.

In homage to waste, we called our 1-acre project and the blog we started to track its development *Holy Scrap*.

When we were ready to build a new structure, we started with a list.

OUR NEW BUILDING MUST...

BE BUILT BY PEOPLE NO STRONGER OR MORE SKILLFUL THAN WE ARE

BE MADE MOSTLY OUT OF WASTE

BE ENERGY-EFFICIENT, REQUIRING VERY LITTLE HEATING OR COOLING

COST LESS THAN $5,000   LAST A LONG TIME

The first thing we did was learn how to use SketchUp, a computer-aided design (CAD) program that we downloaded free from the Internet. SketchUp enabled us to create sophisticated technical drawings and communicate with structural engineers. Once a structural engineer approved our papercrete designs (after two revisions and at the cost of $50), we sent the approved blueprints to the state, where they joined an archive of approved building techniques for New Mexico. Once the designs were state-approved, our local building inspector was relieved of all liability. We were free to build papercrete domes.

Right away we published our dome design on the Internet and encouraged others to use it for free. The days of corporations patenting Mikey's ideas were over. We celebrated.

The first dome we built is 10 feet in diameter and has a 13-foot apex. We started it with a rebar and metal lath armature. Pumping papercrete slurry into the space between interior and exterior armatures made foot-thick walls when it dried. With a stucco sprayer made for papercrete, we applied another paper-based mix modified for outdoor conditions and mixed in an umber powder for color.

~ Papercrete ~

Papercrete is easy to work with, made of readily available waste material, and insulates well.
We published the plan for this 10-foot-diameter by 13-foot-high dome on the internet to encourage others to use it for free

Design a structure using sketchUp

Build a jig

Make a rebar armature

Skin the inner and outer walls of the armature with metal lath

Make a papercrete slurry and pump into the space between the interior and exterior lath to make foot-thick walls

To finish, spray a papercrete mix over the interior and exterior walls.

Today the 10-foot-diameter dome holds the batteries and inverters for the PV solar array that produces all of our power. The second papercrete building is a more ambitious 20-foot-diameter dome with a 16-foot apex. It includes a washroom and a loft. When finished, it will house guests.

We transformed our land by remodeling a mobile home that most people would have thrown away, planting gardens and trees, installing a PV solar array, and building papercrete domes.

Life in Truth or Consequences, New Mexico, in 2008, when we were building our domes, could be summed up by the slogan someone in town printed on T-shirts: *Camp T or C.* The young retirees and 30- to 40-something-year-olds that we'd met at the coffee shop before moving to town regularly visited our building project, and we visited theirs. Everyone borrowed tools, exchanged ideas, and occasionally got in inner tubes and floated down the Rio Grande. There were barbecues and parties, art openings, desert hikes, and gatherings around fire pits. Very few people had traditional professional jobs. Most were either self-employed or building something that might one day produce income. Never was there the feeling of needing to rush. Life was good in Camp T or C.

Eventually we decided that we weren't cut out for running a bed and breakfast or eco hotel, so we scrapped our business plan and Holy Scrap became our home and life lab. We kept building because it had become our pleasure to do so. We continued to build small earthy-looking domes that don't need much heating or cooling and imagined that one would become a kitchen, another a bedroom, a living room, or even a guest room. The only problem inherent in the design is that it might be hard to find our two cats.

And not a day passed without our feeling that we had achieved something, solved a problem, advanced an idea, dreamed a dream, or got something remodeled, built, and made. We approached problems with a willing-to-try attitude, knowing that failure could be remedied by calling in a professional. With the aid of YouTube and websites that feature tutorials, there is no reason not to give every new thing a try. This attitude makes it less scary to start even the most ambitious of projects.

Free Fuel

Imagination is more important than knowledge. For knowledge
is limited to all we now know and understand while imagination
embraces the entire world, and all there ever will be to know and
understand.

— ALBERT EINSTEIN

Lots of people who live in T or C say the reason they do is that their
vehicle broke down here. Jesse, the amazing jack-of-all-trades who
helped us remodel our house and who apologizes each time he per-
forms a feat of strength, drives a diesel-burning European city bus that
he converted into a roaming carpenter's shop. Scott teaches students
at a community college in northern New Mexico to convert Fieros
into rocket-fast electric cars. Our neighbor rocks out to the sound of
the band Journey while he restores Fieros, none of which will become
electric vehicles. Shayna gave birth to Levi in a Subaru in the Home
Depot parking lot in Las Cruces. To save the life of a breatharian who
was starving to death, Andy Potter drove Mikey and me across a river
in his Land Rover. Larry the luthier drives a pickup with the wings of a
Cadillac welded to it. He tells great stories about driving hundred-dollar
Caddies on off-road trails in Montana and driving past hesitant people
in 4x4s afraid to go any farther. Rob can be seen around town driving a red scooter; his other vehicle is his home and has two dogs and a
seasonal girlfriend in it. Jason the scrapper is always driving a different
junky vehicle and siphons gas out of scrap cars before he gathers them
up and sells them by the pound.

Local ranchers favor white diesel pickup trucks with dual suspension. There are five electric vehicles in town. Ladies who meet up at

Scott with a Fiero he modified into a fast electric car.

yard sales on Saturday drive four of them. Mikey and I drive the fifth. We got ours from Jason the scrapper in exchange for papercrete blocks and some cash. Alyce and Julian live on 10 acres in a 150-square-foot trailer designed to mount on the back of a pickup truck. They built 500 square feet of screened porch around it. Luke rode to our house on a bike he bought at a Walmart that he walked to from the El Paso airport. One hundred and twenty miles later, he taught a bike repair workshop at our house, then rode the bike back to Walmart and returned it in better condition than he bought it in. From Walmart, he walked back to the El Paso airport and flew home to Austin.

Mikey and I also have an old electric golf cart we use for moving things around our homestead. We traded hundreds of papercrete blocks for it. Gavio remodeled the inside of an Airstream by adding mud adobe walls and a stove made of clay. Nick, a.k.a. Smoke, drives a 14-foot

U-Haul box truck, because when he went to rent it he found that it was cheaper to buy it. A boy band burning WVO in a grease-converted rented van stopped at our place to buy some biofuel. They gave Mikey their new CD and told him, "It's not very good."

A tiny, well-made, wood-shingled home complete with front door, mailbox, doorbell, and lantern was perched on the back of a pickup and parked around town for a while. A bus covered in quotes from the Bible was parked in front of what used to be the only bar downtown (now there are none) until a local called the cops and somehow related

Our two electric vehicles include a junky golf cart and little EV we got in a trade. They are handy for trips to the river to collect sand for the garden.

the vehicle to homeland security. It was removed. Many sawed-off or stretched-out vehicles made of parts of one vehicle welded to seemingly incompatible parts of another regularly pass through town.

Our neighbor Brian uses his short bus to go to Vansteader gatherings, get-togethers for nomads who live in their vans and tour around the country. His motorcycle has a sidecar used exclusively by his dog Dina. A family of three that sells handmade goods at craft fairs lives in a full-size WVO-burning school bus. We couldn't shake off an ornery hippie couple who wanted to park their bus on our property. They had once lived at the Beehive Collective in Maine and were hauling a sewing studio, a drum kit, a pottery kiln, a motorcycle, two bikes, a canoe, and a library. A nice bunch of kids planned to sell the workers building the spaceport's runway ice cream and coffee from their bus. On their way out to the spaceport, they hit a cow, which broke the bus. After buying the cow from the rancher who owned it, they had no money for fuel and could not get to the spaceport to sell their ice cream and coffee. They were stuck in town for months.

Media mogul Ted Turner owns much of the land north and south of T or C, where he raises buffalo, wolves, and Bolson tortoises and drives an old faded-yellow Suburban. Jay and Rhonda used to lend an antique wooden railway caboose for a night or two to folks passing through until they sold it to Chas and Cat, who do craniosacral therapy using real dolphins. Michael and Tess are building a hot-spring resort in town and have a van covered with images of a mythic deity called Green Tara.

Many of these vehicles would fit right into the scene in *Mad Max Thunderdome*, when the auctioneer of Bartertown describes a stolen cart pulled by camels that he is trying to hock by boasting that it has "independent suspension, power steering, and no emissions!"

The vehicle that changed *our* lives was a vegetable-oil-burning school bus turned mobile broadcast news center driven by nomad filmmaker and media activist Flux Rostrum.

I opened the giant sheet-metal gates that make our compound feel like a place from which Willy Wonka might emerge to let in the school bus. Though Wonka himself may not be making an appearance, Mikey does well as a substitute when he emerges from the unusual rounded gate wearing a silk-screened zip-up jumpsuit, driving our truck with a papercrete mixer in tow.

Flux's giant bus gurgled and spurted like diesel engines do. It rolled hesitatingly onto the lot and landed in front of power post #11 with what seemed to be its very last bit of energy. Our property's RV hookups were proving useful. Vehicles seem to have a natural homing mechanism that helps them find the posts. With no instruction, they pull up to the lifeless toadstools, cool their engines, and express their need.

Flux Rostrum spilled out of his bus to meet me.

"Tryin' to keep the good clothes clean?" I gestured to the apron that he wore on top of an outfit that was at least as filthy as the apron.

He smiled and gave me a dirty hug.

Flux fills his media-center-on-wheels with grease from a nearby restaurant after he and Mikey fixed the rig.

I had not seen Flux since we met in a Brooklyn coffee shop called Fix years earlier. Back then he could still pass for a journalist, go on job interviews, and seem believable when holding up a press badge. Since then Flux had given his life to a media subculture. In the broadcast-center-on-wheels that was his current home, he traveled the country documenting underreported events such as messy union battles in sparsely populated American cities. He interviewed veterans who were denied benefits or ostracized for warning a new generation of young soldiers about what was to come. He covered student protests, the eviction of nonprofits, and struggles in the lives of poor people. He filmed racial discrimination battles that did not have enough marketing hooks for the mainstream media to care about.

Once Flux's bus was inside our gate, it did what all buses do when they arrive on our property: it stopped working. As it turned out, Flux had just bought the rig and the WVO fuel system was already giving him problems. Thus the dirty apron and the equally dirty clothes below it. The life of a greaser is a messy one. The complications were many, but Flux was in the right spot. Mikey was more than a little excited to survey the rig and troubleshoot the issues: a sump pump that didn't have what it took to move the heavy fuel, a variety of clogged filters, not enough heat to thin the fuel, and a bottom-dollar system that just kind of sucked.

Four days later Flux was on the road again and sputtering down I-25. I believe his next stop was Slab City, in the desert in Southern California. That night Mikey came into the house after an extra-long stint in his shipping-container lab in the yard. He wore a guilty expression for 3 a.m.

He posed the rhetorical question "Guess what?"

"What?" I barked, hearing my mother's Bronx accent.

"I bought a Mercedes on eBay. A diesel!"

MICROBATCH INGREDIENTS
4 gallons waste vegetable oil (WVO)
½ gallon methanol
60 grams lye

With fluctuating fuel costs, an energy crisis anticipated, and a waste product readily available to us, fuel was already on our list of things to make ourselves. The day had arrived.

Get on your apron, I thought.

With the help of a local mechanic who boasted a gang tattoo inside his lip and worked to the soundtrack of "Sweet Home Alabama," we successfully installed a grease conversion kit in our "new" Mercedes. Within a couple of months we were burning straight filtered WVO. A couple of years later we added another diesel car to our fleet, an older-model red VW Beetle that has not given us much trouble. Instead of converting the Beetle, we produce homemade biofuel for it; we found

If I hadn't pushed Chance, our WVO-burning car, up the hill, we would have been stuck in the desert all night.

that making biofuel is preferable to running a car converted to run straight WVO. Lesson learned.

We named the Mercedes from El Paso, Texas, Chance because there was only a chance that it would get us anywhere. As those chances seemed to lessen, we modified its name to Fat Chance. When it was roadside and waiting for a tow truck to come get it, it was No Chance. Last Chance was what I called the car when I put my foot down and told Mikey that we had to sell it. This came just after an incident that took place many miles from the nearest town, just after I gave Chance a push to get it uphill while Mikey pumped the gas pedal. Once the car was over the crest of the hill, with the passenger door hanging open, Mikey shouted, "Get in!" and it was my task to complete the uphill jaunt and hop into the moving car, lest it lose its steam again and slide backward down the steep slope. We called the car Only Chance when, for various reasons, our other cars were not available and we had to drive it. To Mikey and Chance's credit, the breakdowns had to do with Chance's being old and crappy — rarely did they have anything to do with the grease conversion kit or the burning of WVO. Chance is now a beach car that we use almost exclusively to go to the lake and back again. It seems that the threat to sell it caused Chance to pull himself together. Chance is running still.

But in our main car, the red VW Beetle, we get 30 to 50 miles per gallon burning biodiesel fuel, which costs us only about a dollar a gallon to make. Trips to the grocery, to the homes of friends in town, to the hardware store, to garage sales, to parties, to the bowling alley, to restaurants, are free in our electric car, which we power off our PV solar array. I no longer make trips to gas stations.

Things of value

Mikey hung up the phone and paced agitatedly in the kitchen.

He had been talking to someone from his old job who had wanted to know why he was cashing out his 401k account. Mikey explained that he did not trust the stock market. "I'm going to use the money I have to invest in the life I am living right now," he told the befuddled rep.

"He thought I was crazy and wanted to help me *find* equity," Mikey said as he rolled his eyes.

How does one *find* equity? It seemed so abstract. Equity is not unearthed from a tomb on an archeological dig; it does not emerge from a dusty box at a garage sale. You can't hold it. The banks made it seem as though it could be produced from thin air — as long as you owned something worth money, like a home.

A trick of the world of capital, we decided. A way to detach money from something valuable and make it, as they say, liquid. I figured *equity* was a code word that meant "easier to steal." Bankers were doing this kind of thing with homes all over the country as people were offered giant mortgages and then foreclosed on. "Not us," we vowed.

In 2008 the market became volatile. We watched it rise and fall as it had done in years past, only now it was even more erratic, the changes more extreme. Sometimes its fluxuations were due to real circumstances in the world, such as a bone-dry rainy season in Florida causing a spike in the price of oranges. But all too often the swings of the market seemed tied to the mysterious workings of a world to which we were not privy. Financial products too complex to figure out (even, as would later be clear, by those who sold them) shifted and re-formed the lives of real people, making some rich and others poor. Never did the activity make the overall conditions for life any better.

Since the dramatic game does not make common sense, we opted out entirely: we took all the money we had and made it *liquid*. No more stocks, no investments. We put it in a plain old savings account that earned 2 percent interest. According to all the experts, the professional money managers, bankers, and the like, we did the dumbest thing possible. But when Lehman Brothers went bankrupt, Bear Stearns collapsed, and the whole economy went haywire, it didn't seem dumb to us. I thought of something I'd heard the Sufis say: *Life lives; only death dies.* Well, the nation's dying banking system had never contained life.

In addition to getting out of the stock market and cashing in our retirement accounts, we decided to get rid of all the money we had by swapping it for things that we thought would have value in spite of economic conditions. Things that sustain life: land, water, tools, and equipment. *Buy things that make other things* became our mantra.

While we still had some money, we asked ourselves, half jokingly, "What do we need for a Mad Max world?" "The best blender!" I decided, one night cozied up in bed with my laptop. Food was on the essential list, along with shelter, fuel, and power. I chose a model with a high-power motor that seconded as a hammer mill so that we could use it to make cornmeal and nut and grain flours. And I got one with a rebuilt motor and a lifetime warranty for half the price of a new one.

We bought tools and materials to build just about anything: a concrete mixer, a mortar mixer, a welder, levels, a wood planer, electric weed whackers, a scythe, a paint sprayer, impact drills — things that before living in New Mexico I'd never heard of. We got rid of tools that had two-cycle gas engines and replaced them with electric versions that could be powered by the clean energy produced by our own PV solar system.

Pasta Maker

COOK!

DUTCH OVEN

BUILD!

WOOD PLANER

DRILL

ANGLE GRINDER

BUY THINGS THAT MAKE OTHER THINGS

FRUIT TREE

OBD (ON BOARD DEVICE) SCAN TOOL

FIX!

SOLDERING IRON

High-Powered Blender

SEWING MACHINE

MEND

We crammed our new investments into a moderately dented metal shipping container that was no longer suitable for carrying international cargo but made an excellent shed, and remodeled a second shipping container into an electronics lab for Mikey to work in. Dreaming aloud, as we had promised to do from a hot tub under a star-soaked sky on our first trip to T or C, Mikey wanted to bury his metal lab in the yard like Luke Skywalker's home on Tatooine in the original *Star Wars*. Our water table was too high for that. He'd make do.

Our shipping container gave us 160 square feet of space for less money than a flimsy shed purchased at a hardware store. And it will last for decades.

The Notorious Goblins

Opportunity may knock only once, but temptation leans on the doorbell.
— Author Unknown

During the first two years that we lived in the desert, we earned money here and there from bits of work that promised not to steal too much time from building and developing our property. I began a column that I wrote for *Craft* magazine that I called Re:Fitted. For *Craft*'s readers, I reported on creative people who found interesting ways to work with reuse. I taught yoga and shared Sufi meditations with a group of students, and I managed the growing network of Swap-O-Rama-Rama events that had sprung up. Some of these activities brought about small infusions of cash that staved off our going entirely broke.

Then civilization showed up armed with its most notorious goblins: fame and money. I had already considered Swap-O-Rama-Rama's future, so I was not entirely unprepared for the temptation the goblins dangled before me. I knew the options: renting huge stadiums in big cities, hiring staff, producing and managing the events, and copyrighting the name. I could make a good living franchising Swap-O-Rama-Rama. Bizarre Bazaar, the Renegade Craft Faire, and Maker Faire were doing this very thing with their variety of what they had to offer.

Swap-O-Rama-Rama came about as the result of a pledge, a promise to create a remedy for the lust for stuff. To commodify it by turning it into a money-generating business felt like the breaking of a sacred trust. The idea (the pledge) had more value than its offspring (Swap-O-Rama-Rama). Living in Burning Man's Black Rock City had showed me that the value of what I created could only be secured by making it a gift. The fame and money goblins would have to find another candidate.

Still, my ego let out a bratty cry: "*I* want to be successful." It was a dramatic scene. Network TV producers started to call. The same month, nine publishers called with opportunities to write a book. "Wouldn't a book and a TV show turn *me* into a product?" I asked Mikey. At that time, it would have. Then one of the largest utility companies in the country asked me to produce a Swap-O-Rama-Rama with its name on it. The company dangled $100,000, a fee to wash over its bad reputation with my good one.

With a head heavy with decisions to make, I went into town to grab lunch and think over the temptations. A woman who promoted jazz in Chicago before moving to New Mexico and whom I had seen around town leaned over to me from the neighboring table. Through ostentatious sunglasses her spirit rose up with the cane that she waved in the air. As though our encounter were an undercover rendezvous, she lowered her chin, then raised her eyes over the gaudy frames to meet mine and said, "People think they come to this town for healing and relaxation. That's what I thought, too, and look what happened to me!"

As the volume of her voice increased, so did the height of her cane. She lifted her pant leg to expose what was below: a prosthetic foot strapped to a shortened lower leg. An accident? What had happened? The fake was adorned with a trendy sneaker and an adorable lace-edged sock.

"Don't forget the name, dearie, Truth *or* Consequences."

The delivery of advice was foreboding. I imagined that if the universe had employees, the one who worked in the department of pledge-keeping was standing over me.

"Okay, I get it," I said to the imaginary steward. I must not commodify what I created.

When I got home I conjured the image of Luke Skywalker in the scene in *Star Wars* when he has to trust and then use the force to bring about the empire's demise. With a battle cry, I replied to the TV producers: No. To the nine publishers: No. And to the power company and its $100,000: No.

After passing through this test I was ready to release Swap-O-Rama-Rama to the world as a gift. I just needed a way to do it that ensured that it remain decommodified. The tools that civilization offered for the task did not seem a right fit: copyrights, patents, and the model of the franchise.

I turned to nature with the imaginary keys in hand. Sitting between my own two lush garden beds, I imagined the feeling of hot water rising up from the geothermal springs below me and tuned my hearing to the flocks of birds that traversed overhead and were traveling to places as far as Siberia. A blue heron impressed me with the size of its wingspan just before I closed my eyes. The air smelled of nothing in particular. *Clean,* I thought. The sun shone hot and bright, and I reminded myself that because of it, my sustenance grows. The food I eat lives because of photosynthesis. I am a carrier of the transmuted light. I dissolved the boundary of my small self and broadened my sense of who I thought myself to be until I was the size of the whole planet. Then I brought up the question in order to view it anew.

What if I build a ship, the first of its kind, a marvel of good design? Before taking credit for it, I would have to admit that the history of shipbuilding had played a part in my success. To build my ship I have to borrow from the knowledge that accumulated over time. It wasn't I who figured out how to join one piece of wood to another or how to sew a sail. I did not provide the trees that the wood came from. I could never invent a tree or muster one up from scratch. I can't make wind or buoyancy so that things can float. Creating water is beyond my skill set.

When I *own* an idea and take credit for it, my ship, what is it that I am taking credit for? From this expanded view I could see that I ought to *give* credit, not take it.

Copyrights and patents are devices of civilization that have creative people thinking, *This is my last good idea.* After all, if people believed that another good idea was coming, that they were essentially creative and full of ideas, they wouldn't bother to concretize the one they'd just had with a copyright or a patent. Our culture had us thinking, *I'm not really creative — it was a fluke that I had this one good idea.* Essentially copyrights and patents turn creators into security guards of their ideas; they transform revelatory experiences into redundancy, and creativity into product. The systems our civilization has conjured prevent the best of our ideas from being released into the world so that they can be shaped and shared by others.

Luckily a new type of *open* license has sprung up. People are using the Creative Commons to protect and share their good ideas. For Swap-O-Rama-Rama, I chose a Creative Commons license that enables people, nonprofit organizations, and communities to share and use it, and I excluded for-profits from use. I vowed to be its gatekeeper.

Nevertheless, with Swap-O-Rama-Rama's continued growth, the pestering goblins returned. Swap-O-Rama-Rama was starting to look like a strange oracle.

One day a woman who organized a Swap-O-Rama-Rama in the Midwest presented me with a unique conundrum. In her crew of volunteers, whom she described as mostly struggling and unemployed artists, a woman who seemed well-off insisted on getting paid. The organizer asked me, "What do I tell her?"

Her situation helped me notice that there is a kind of poverty that is different from the suffering that comes from not having what is fundamental to life. There is a kind of poverty that comes from having enough and not knowing it.

Some people try to prove that the world is one of lack by asking it for what they know it will not give them. After all, who asks to get paid for volunteering except someone who expects to hear, "There is not enough"? If this volunteer were to experience life anew, she needed a different answer from the one she was expert at eliciting.

Instead of telling her, "No. Volunteers don't get paid," we said, "Yes," and added, "Here is a little more than you asked for."

Months later the organizer called to tell me that the advice had worked: the woman whom she paid at the first event had volunteered at the second, no questions asked.

Before I could exhale, the goblins were at my door once more. I heard that a car manufacturer was planning and promoting Swap-O-Rama-Rama events in 14 cities in the United States. The company planned to use the events to market a new car that had mediocre mileage, a greenwash. Unlike the usual Swap-O-Rama-Rama, which created the new out of the donated used clothes of those who attended, the proposed events would let people make things out of new clothing that the company provided. Since the company executives had not asked my permission to use Swap-O-Rama-Rama, they did not know that for-profit entities were excluded from its Creative Commons license.

This is when I first saw the power of the commons. The car manufacturer had spent over $100,000 arranging for the events. At the same time, Swap-O-Rama-Rama was being produced by communities all over the world on a budget of nearly zero, run on volunteer energy and free materials from the waste stream.

Shutting the mimic down was satisfying. I could hardly believe I'd won a fight against a giant corporation. But still I wondered how these things happen. A cookie-crumb trail led me to the marketing company and the woman responsible for the sale. I typed her name into a search engine and learned that she was also a textile artist. In the same way that I had set aside what I thought was right in order to succeed at my job, I imagined that her profession had led her to express her interest

in Swap-O-Rama-Rama in an inappropriate way. When I invited her to teach a workshop at the next swap in New York, she accepted. When we met there, we did not discuss the car company or the blunder. We made things.

I turned my gaze to meet the long view of the mountains that, like sturdy grandparents, gazed back at me through the kitchen window. The white light outside bounced off a blue sky and beamed brightly and everywhere. I had no idea how I would earn the income I needed to live in New Mexico, but I knew that it was not to come from fearing a lack of money.

I remembered the promise Mikey and I had made in a hot tub along the Rio Grande. I was here to dream aloud. The concepts of acculturated life — money and fame — were too heavy to take flight in the Land of Enchantment.

Remember that money is the most abundant and least precious thing on earth.

The Cost of Living

The merchant in Love's bazaar is none other than the customer
himself. Where then is the profit in trying to buy and sell?

— Javad Nurbakhsh

While I battled the fame and money goblins, Mikey was earning money
blogging for media outlets like *Popular Science* and Hack a Day. He did
online Linux consulting and sold filtered WVO when there was extra.
Freelance work led him to design custom equipment for various New
Mexico algae companies. But things got really exciting when he began
designing his own electronic devices to make living our postconsumer
life easier.

It was our domestic life that made it even more obvious to us than
it had been when we'd first written on our whiteboard in New York
Having a job is expensive. Though building a home out of waste and
making our own fuel and power had freed us from a couple of commerce's main entanglements, we still had fixed costs that could not be
paid with a Bundt cake: a mortgage, a gas bill, and taxes, to name a few.

Growing and wildcrafting food and medicine showed us how
precious our domestic life is to us. We became fermenters and began
producing wine, mead, kimchi, cheese, bread, yogurt, tempeh, and kombucha at home. With all of these labors taking place in our own abode,
taking up all our time, having a job was a direct threat to the quality of
our life. Too much time freelancing or — worse — a full-time gig could
end our diet of homegrown organic food produced by our garden and
the raw cheeses that we made from fresh milk each week. It could put
us back at the pump buying petroleum fuel. If we tried to build even
one building project with a licensed crew doing the labor, we'd have

gone broke the first year we were in New Mexico. We were wealthy *because* we did not have jobs.

Over time, our home economy became nuanced and took on a particular rhythm. As much as possible, we reduced our reliance on what required money and increased our participation in the local non-monetary economy. Mikey was the first to detect and plug into the local domestic economy in T or C. He started baking and giving away bread. As he did, our friendships flourished and people started giving him things in return. As we learned to make more things we gave better gifts: homemade wine, salve, teas, and plant medicines.

When we started a cottage industry, I told Mikey that it felt to me as though we had started a production facility to make gifts that we also put online in the form of a store, just in case someone who didn't live near us wanted to have them. As I learned at Black Rock City and confirmed at Swap-O-Rama-Rama, handmade objects are imbued with meaning; they have real value. They contain stories, heart, intention, and responsibility. And as gifts, their value goes up exponentially. The things we made were gifts first. We distributed them to friends in our community. The little extra we made we put online. They were commodities second.

As in many small towns, the local domestic economy in T or C functions outside of the national monetary system and runs on favors, labor, advice (good, bad, and otherwise), and objects gifted and bartered: camel poo, pies, fabric, baskets, blocks, building materials, and furniture (to name a few). Between friends and locals, an exchange of money is the low road. Though there is an exception to this point of etiquette: Almost everyone does one thing for money. We know what each other's one thing is, and for it we happily pay each other in American dollars. This is how we support one another and how we recognize the tie we all have to the national economy, which, for now, still exists.

Sensing and participating in an unspoken law of reciprocity, we volunteer on local projects, such as building a solar hot-air heater for an elderly man in the neighborhood. We sit on boards for proposed food buying groups and co-ops. For a while we moderated a renewable energy group. Occasionally we produce events such as the Better Living Through Experimentation talk, musical events, clothing swaps, and a weeklong homesteading skill-sharing workshop for homesteaders around the country. Mikey taught a class on the subject of power and batteries to a group of eight students, none of whom was over 12 years old.

We arrived in the desert with some savings to lean on, and lean we did. Truth or Consequences's low cost of living helped us bide the time needed to tease out questions like *Is there a way to live that does not need money? Can we discover it before running out of money?* Before two years were up, we were no longer people who required six-figure incomes to live, but people who led a happier and more abundant life on a combined income of under $30,000 a year, a year of rent in Manhattan.

The only thing that Mikey and I gave up during our quest for a decommodified life was broad-coverage medical insurance. Once in New Mexico, we reduced our medical insurance plan to one that covers only catastrophic events that cost more than a few thousand dollars. We pay approximately a hundred dollars a month per person for this level of insurance. There were many reasons that we made this choice. We wanted to know that a large medical event could not break us. But otherwise, we were also hesitant to rely on insurance companies, especially when we learned that many of them have been convicted of criminal behavior.

Instead of investing money in an insurance company, we decided to invest our time in health and to pay ourselves. Our health insurance plan consists of our organic garden, local wild-game meats, wildcrafted medicines we make from local plants, pollution-free high desert air far away from industry, life in rhythm with nature, stress-free living without deadlines and traffic, inspiration, a sense of purposefulness, and physical exercise from work and play. Our lifestyle *is* our insurance plan.

Before we left New York, we relieved ourselves of debt and promised each other that we would never acquire new debt. But we did acquire new debt in New Mexico. We could not find a way to buy property and a home without a mortgage. We also couldn't get a mortgage. Banks don't loan money to unemployed people in their thirties who admit the goal of *never having a job again*. In retrospect, this was a hidden blessing. To get around the technicality, we found a property being sold by a person willing to hold the mortgage at a low interest rate. It was debt nonetheless, and we added it to our cost-of-living chart.

In the same week we were inspired by both Al Gore's film *An Inconvenient Truth* and the film *The End of Suburbia*, and we took the cash we had left in our savings account and bought a 2-kilowatt PV solar system and a bank of batteries. On April 23, 2008, we went off-grid. We hedged our bet that in the future everything dependent on petroleum — food, fuel, and power — would go up in price and become harder to obtain.

When the stock market finally crashed and the banks were bailed out, I read reports that parks in Los Angeles were turning into tent cities that housed those who'd lost their homes. Meanwhile, the stores in Truth or Consequences remained open and continued doing what they knew well: selling inexpensive used junk. As foreclosure rates jumped around the country, I noticed that in southern New Mexico less than 1 percent of the homes had been foreclosed on. New Mexico had been poor for a long time; people lived off the waste stream and resided in old mobile homes and trailers that they already owned. Life went on as usual.

WENDY AND MIKEY'S
YEARLY COST OF LIVING*

SHELTER
- Mortgage, home insurance, and property taxes $9,100
- Natural gas (for home) $275
- Electric $120 (basic connection; we keep a grid tie in case we need it, such as during a rare cloudy week or to equalize our battery bank)
- Water/sewer/trash (combined in Truth or Consequences) $1,200

TECHNOLOGY/COMMUNICATIONS
- Internet provider $600
- Two cell phones with data plans $1,320

TRANSPORTATION
- Insurance: four vehicles $600
- Vehicle registration $200
- Fuel $300 (10,000 miles per year)

FOOD/HEALTH
- Health insurance (catastrophic only) $2,400
- Food and domestic goods $4,500

TOTAL COST OF LIVING
Just over $20,000 annual fixed expenses

*2011 figures

Take Time

Time is short. That's the first thing. . . . Time is a servant if you
are its master. Time is your god if you are its dog. We are the
creators of time, the victims of time, and the killers of time. Time
is timeless. That's the second thing. You are the clock.
— WILLEM DAFOE AS AN ANGEL IN THE FILM *Faraway, So Close!*

In New Mexico, we became money-poor and time-wealthy. I'd take
time over money any day. (Who wouldn't, really?) People who have
money often use it to buy time.

Time away from unnatural schedules like the standard 9 to 5 allows
your body to regain its natural rhythm. Waking, sleeping, working,
resting, playing, eating, and contemplating have their own time, and
that time is different for each of us. Some say that the hunter-gatherer
lifestyle used time in fits and starts, that people in those cultures worked
hard for short periods, rested, and played. Personal rhythms connect
people to large natural rhythms such as circadian and seasonal cycles.
Connecting to these rhythms produces the feeling of being connected
to life. Because these systems are natural, rejoining them brings about a
feeling of well-being.

- Imagine having time to see what happens when you have time.
- The soul is slow. Having time makes this evident.
- Earmark the time passing now by noticing what is dawning.
- Have you had the time to discover what you love to do?

IT TAKES TIME . . .

- to get to know people. You cannot love what you do not know.
- to make things that represent no monetary gain but that improve life: gifts, toys, and things for pleasure alone.
- to grow healthy food, cook, prepare, and savor it.
- to fix what breaks.
- to learn new skills.
- to get past representation and arrive at presence.

WITH TIME . . .

- you can wake up in the middle of the night to witness astral events like meteor showers and eclipses.
- you can get to know yourself.
- you can custom-fit your clothing.
- you can customize your world and make everything the right size, shape, color, and style for you.
- you can call in product warranties and guarantees. Starting a conversation with the words "I'm unemployed" tells customer service reps that you have time to see your complaint through.
- you can transform free raw materials and waste into valuable goods.
- you can listen instead of hear and can see instead of look.
- you may discover what having time leads to.

Getting Better All the Time

When we assert our claim that this existence is blessed it gives
us a relaxed assurance and holds back the floodgates of despair.
— GAYAN MACHER

Life in the waste stream is like life in an arranged marriage. When
things go well, one is immediately lifted from a set point of moderate expectation. I consider the sleek aluminum-framed couch from the
1950s that I found teetering in an easy-to-reach spot in the landfill and
liken the treasure to the joy experienced with each sign of a good trait
discovered in a not-yet-familiar spouse. A kind act, a generous deed,
a dimple previously unnoticed adds a sweet charm and improves a
matrimonial partner's likability. Good junk is a constant upgrade from
something unknown or mediocre to something better.

In my twenties, when my professional life was at its start and a
future career in marketing was ahead of me, I used a calculator to
estimate my life's earnings, based on the standard wages for my occupa-
tion. I crunched the numbers over decades, the span of my work life,
and ended the calculation at retirement. I fattened the math with the
occasional bonus and considered the value of the extras that working
people trade for their time and creativity, things like medical benefits
and fresh titles that indicate more responsibility and more time spent. I
compared the high and low salaries earned in my field. I sank, realizing
that the numbers revealed a future of few surprises, a life that thrived
on continuity. With planned joy neatly slotted for weekends, I knew

that this was not the life I was meant to live. It is a different vision of forward movement than things always getting better.

Between building projects, I cushion outdoor couch frames with newish foam pads that I upholster with sturdy shade cloth. Solid iron springs in steampunk shapes and parts from long-gone farm machines are regularly celebrated treasures that stand here and there in our yard like postapocalyptic art. To me they are part of a collage of reuse that signals a coming renaissance. After the waste is used up and industry slowed, I imagine we will all become makers of things. Waste buys us time to learn.

Rusty saw blades make pretty wind chimes when strung side by side with baling wire along dried yucca stalks. Stackable plastic bread trays from the back of an out-of-business grocery make an excellent drying rack for herbs, fruits, and veggies.

Cordless power tools constantly turn up in the trash, their only flaw a dead battery that finds inspiration to live a little longer after being zapped with a welder. Nearly free thrift-shop furniture — sanded, stained, and re-knobbed — warms our home. The goods that surround me shine with achievement. Refurbishing is as relaxing to me as I imagine knitting must be for the crafters who stitch together colorful strands of yarn while riding the New York subways.

As new and better junk is found, old, less great junk is dumped back where it came from — except, having been used a while longer, it prevented something else from being manufactured and new materials from being mined. Fewer people drove, printed things on paper, and wrote it all down. Fewer of us missed the color of the sky that day. The dog got an extra walk. *Things are always getting better.*

Some of the pitfalls of consumerism can still be found in the waste stream. Namely, the tendency to hoard. Mikey and I occasionally bump into waste-stream hoarders who fill homes, empty lots, extra buildings, and storage containers with stuff. They boast stories of projects they are going to build one day when there are future resources such as energy and inspiration. Far away from cities and shopping malls, the belief in lack persists and drives people to acquire more than they need.

A belief in an unseen law of reciprocity prevents us from doing the same. I imagine the invisible employee of the universe's department of pledge-keeping standing over me, telling me that if I take more than I need or acquire out of fear, the abundance may stop. Even if abundance is the actual condition of the world, we still must come out to meet it. With this in mind, I regularly review the neatly arranged junk piles that we keep divided in categories: wood, R-panel, flat metal scraps, metal and PVC pipe, fabric, and natural fiber. I thin the piles and pass on to others what has not been put to use.

My favorite activity for reducing waste is droplifting, an activity that Mikey and I engage in annually, dressed as Christmas elves. Droplifting in the guise of a holiday elf requires six things: an elf costume, social bravery, the ability to size people up, some junk, a belief in abundance, and joy. After rummaging through all the drawers and cabinets in our house, we stuff an odd lot of goods no longer useful to us into a fire-engine-red fleece Santa sack lined with white faux fur. With our red jumpers trimmed in the same fur, our snowflake buttons, and pointy hoods, we *are* elves.

"I bet you would like a present," I whispered to a shy country girl who stood at hip height next to her daddy on the main drag in town. It was a week before Christmas and Broadway was closed for the night, the yellow lines dividing the road dotted with metal fire drums similar to the ones I'd made at the Brooklyn metal shop. Noticing the dad's tall ten-gallon hat, I imagined him in a dual-suspension pickup truck and handed him a free-car-wash coupon. I winked at him while handing his daughter a colorful set of stickers. Her eyes widened as she considered if I might be a real elf from the North Pole. I told her that she could be sure that I was, because only a real elf can play the nose flute. That's where my $1 plastic nose flute comes in handy.

I gave a cold woman a fuzzy scarf I'd picked up at a San Francisco Swap-O-Rama-Rama and handed a set of earmuffs to a shivering cop. It mattered very little to us that we happened to have been raised Jewish and were acting as elves in a town where our tribe was too thin to form a minyan. "Abundance," I said to Mikey, pointing to the illuminated faces of two kids chomping down on the marshmallows that Mikey had pulled from his sack, handed out, and then helped roast on the open fire.

The best part about droplifting is that items headed for the landfill are transformed into gifts that, I suspect, are less likely to get kicked to the curb, because they've been given by an elf. They are no longer things, and they are more than gifts: they are magical gifts.

The film No Impact Man chronicles a New York family's attempt to live without any impact on the earth. I like No Impact Family. They had a pledge, too — we had that in common. I imagined the movies No Impact Man and The Decommodified Girl playing on a double bill on movie night in Bartertown, the fictitious city in Mad Max. I wondered if the universe had also assigned No Impact Family a mythic creature from the department of pledge-keeping.

This family held steady to their goal in spite of real difficulties. Bravely they gave up life's comforts: air conditioning, electricity, public transportation, and refrigeration, to name a few. At times with strained smiles, they searched out the bright side of the situation.

No Impact Couple maintained demanding professional jobs and an expensive city apartment while at the same time the pledge had them giving up many of the things that made these things tolerable. With a glass-half-full outlook, they appreciated what they could. With their

apartment too hot to bear in the summer months, they enjoyed the extra time they spent in the city's parks. They noted the extra exercise they got from walking instead of riding the subway. They stacked clay pots one inside the other and called the configuration *pot in pot*, a contraption copied from third-world cultures that used the odd formation as a crude form of refrigerated cooling. It didn't work in their New York apartment.

When they gave up riding the subway because it ran on electricity from an energy source that had an impact, I started wondering about context. If a subway is shooting by your home and there is room on it for you, doesn't it make sense to get on? A full subway seems less wasteful than an empty one. The energy has already been spent. When No Impact Family turned off the electricity in their apartment, the scene was bleak. In spite of their high-spiritedness, their lives continuously got more difficult.

I considered No Impact Family's pledge and realized that the pledge itself produced a feeling of lack. Everything in civilization produces an impact, so there was no end to what they had to give up to fulfill their promise. Everywhere they turned, the world had the same answer: *Give up more.*

Over 2,000 miles away in New Mexico, Mikey and I converted a chest freezer to run as a refrigerator using a temperature controller he designed and made, thereby gaining a 10X reduction in the power drawn from our PV solar system. We used the gain to run additional appliances like an air conditioner that is needed during monsoon seasons when swamp coolers have no effect. With many of the lifestyle changes we made, what seemed at first a sacrifice later produced abundance. The only thing Mikey and I really gave up was crappy medical insurance, and we didn't miss that at all (see page 125).

The life Mikey and I were living was abundant because we asked for what could be obtained. We let the world say *yes* to us, instead of inviting it to say *no* by prompting it for what it could not give. No

Impact Family's pledge likened them to the woman who asked the Swap-O-Rama-Rama organizer to pay her to volunteer, even though she knew that volunteers did not get paid. She asked for money and expected to be denied so that she could hear her view of lack confirmed. Civilization can never promise no impact, but nature can promise abundance.

By relying on waste, on what nature provides, and on ourselves, we gave the world a chance to demonstrate abundance. By becoming makers of things, we let our creativity become a transformative link between the free materials available to us and the finished goods that made our lives better.

The momentum of our lives was that things were always getting better. Though the world was essentially the same as it had always been, the same one that No Impact Family and the Swap-O-Rama-Rama volunteer lived in, we experienced abundance. The only thing that changed was that Mikey and I tuned ourselves differently; we made ourselves able to see what had been there all along. I realized that abundance is a truth *and* a point of view. It can be seen only if you come out to meet it.

EVERYONE LIVES IN TWO WORLDS

MODERN CIVILIZATION / NATURE

We are not the same as it; we are living and it is not.

Living. It includes us. We *live* in and make up this world.

Artificially regulated, out of balance

Self-regulating, naturally strives for balance

Produces no waste, a perfect system

Creates waste and causes destruction to life

All activity has to do with the movement of money.

Produces without exertion: water, fire, air, earth; everything needed to make everything

Everything made is a representation of something abstracted from nature.

Can be understood by contemplation. Its knowledge is free and accessible to all. That's why it's called the *common sense*.

Nature is presence, always arising. (It is not representation.)

Requires acculturated knowledge that has to be taught or mimicked but can never been intuited. The knowledge is not guaranteed to be safe or helpful to life.

Driven by an economy that requires consumption

Abundant; always new; creative

Nature is the only sovereign thing; it is reliant on nothing.

Free

Everything is for sale

Civilization is dependent on nature for all its materials

The incomprehensible is solely the result of incomprehension, which seeks what it has and therefore can never make further discoveries.

— Novalis

Nature Unlocked

Each thing in nature is a question containing its own
potential answer.
— Christopher Bamford, *Green Hermeticism: Alchemy & Ecology*

When I was a city dweller, I often wondered about the telluric energy beneath my feet — about gravity, the planet's signature, a force that tethered me to a world of minerals and a hot molten core that spun fast with the giant sphere's rotation. The Sufis taught me to feel it as an expression of love from the planet to the life it hosted. I delight in knowing that I don't really know where I am. I have an address and a zip code on earth, but not among the stars.

In the desert, preparing for a day of foraging, I reflected on the days that Mikey and I used to spend in Central Park. Even though gravity is weaker where we are now at a 4,500-foot elevation, it is easier to feel standing on the parched New Mexico ground than it ever had been in New York City.

Sesame, our 40-pound red heeler with alert shepherd ears and a wide smile, wagged excitedly inside the cab. She knew from the configuration of objects in the truck bed — shovels, buckets, loppers, clippers, and gloves — and the choice of vehicles that we were going on a foraging trip. Few things are more exciting to a native dog than adventures in the desert. She let out a whimper as she paced the cab waiting for us join her.

We packed a picnic lunch that we planned to eat under the canopy of salt cedar trees that guard the bank of the Rio Grande at the spot where it bends toward Caballo Lake. I wanted to check on a stand of mullein, hoping to catch it flowering so that I could make ear oil, a remedy for the swimmer's ear Mikey is prone to in the summer. The plant always flowers within weeks of swimming season.

When we arrived we saw cows trolling the riverbank near our favorite spot. Across the river a sweat lodge I once helped build remained hidden by a tangle of juniper and cedar trees. Walking over to check on the tiny dome of bent willow that I had once covered in thrift-shop blankets, I saw a pile of large lava rocks that still marked the center of the lodge. A dirt circle hard-packed from use could be detected inside the lodge. A larger fire pit for heating the rocks remained just outside the lodge door. Next to it lay a set of antlers for lifting hot stones and moving them from the fire outside to the pit inside. I thought about the sweat lodge leader, who since the last sweat had fallen off the wagon and was wanted by the police for a crime whose details I hoped never to learn. In the Wild West, people sometimes walk a line between terror and transcendence.

I returned to one of the tasks of the day: to gather 10 buckets of sand from the river's edge and to cut enough long, straight salt cedar branches to make the west wall of a shade structure we'd just finished building. After the day's effort we planned to bring the bounty home; mix the sand with clay, compost, and camel poo; and add it to the garden beds in our yard. It was not quite spring and our seed was not yet set, but the mesquite trees threatened to spurt fresh growth and that meant the last frost was near. It was time to prepare for the challenges of spring, such as high winds that might last six or eight weeks, giving struggle to person and plant.

The shade patio had taken us three months to complete. We designed it using SketchUp, then priced, ordered, and scavenged the materials. Each piece of 4-foot metal box tubing was carefully cut with a chop saw and welded together to produce three freestanding arches that, once mounted in the ground and sunk into cement footers, were welded together. Clamps were devised and used to hold them up, levels checked and rechecked, cement mixed. There was the sanding of rough

I love the mix of natural and industrial materials we used to build our patio.

metal edges, welding, and a final coat of Rust-Oleum that we applied reluctantly, weighing its toxicity against the value of what it preserved.

> Compromises come up often. Meet each one with the best knowledge available at the time.

The structure's ceiling was made of lengths of ponderosa pine spaced a few inches apart and tied down by hand with baling wire. As the sun traverses the sky, the pine produces a handsome peekaboo effect of stripes of shade and sun on a stained cement slab below it. I stained the slab a natural earthen color with powdered umber that I mixed with water and stabilized with a cement sealer.

In the summer months, below the ponderosa pine, I hang a giant 20-foot by 12-foot shade cloth that I sewed together in the living room after clearing out almost all the furniture to make room for it. Its canopy diffuses harsh UV rays. The entire structure was made for a few hundred dollars and should stand sturdily in place for decades. I compared it to what that much money could buy — a flimsy premade structure that probably wouldn't last more than a season or two before being destroyed by the wind and left, with fractured legs, next to a dumpster.

Nature is abundant if you know how to look at it. We could have gone to the hardware store and bought a covering for the patio wall, maybe R-panel, but what fun would that have been? Sesame would not have gotten to roam free on the grassy plains and visit the cows by the river, and we would have missed a perfectly good picnic and spring view of the mountains.

In town, mesquite trees drop sweet, protein-rich, caramel-flavored pods on the ground. They are hardly noticed by most, a regular annoyance to some. Mikey and I recognize them as food and wait for the right moment when the trees release the pods with a gentle tug. With cloth sacks we catch the bounty. We choose stands with sweet, fat purple-streaked pods that produce the taste we like best and host the least amount of bugs. (The flat almond-colored variety lacks sweetness and contains a little beetle that survives freezing temperatures and extreme heat.) On daily walks with Sesame we sample still-tethered pods and suck on them to critique their flavor while waiting for the trees to mature. At home, we freeze the loot in a chest freezer for several days and then solar-dry the pods at temperatures over 106°F to ensure that bugs and their eggs are eradicated. When the pods are snap-brittle, we pick through them, breaking off parts where a hole indicates the entry of a critter. Then, with a $1 garage-sale coffee grinder, we turn the cleaned pods into mesquite flour that stores all winter. We make all our baked goods with a ratio of one-third mesquite to two-thirds white (or other) flours. Though mesquite flour sells for 20 times the price of white flour, it is free to us. It requires only awareness, labor, and some time.

Mesquite is an unusual tree. A hardwood nitrogen-fixing legume native to arid regions of the Southwest, it sends out 200-foot taproots to find water. In the worst of droughts, mesquite survives on water too deep to nourish most other trees. Mesquite packs calories in the form of sugar and protein. It is both medicine (topical/internal) and food (flour and molasses): a gluten- and soy-free, high-fiber, calcium-rich treat. The entire pod is edible, with calories that have a balanced amino acid profile.

During summer, the native prickly pear cactus produces a succulent burgundy-red fruit called a tuna, which grows at the end of a thorny green pad. As we do with mesquite, we choose prickly pear cactus plants in advance and watch them mature. Taken early, before the sugars are fully present, the fruit is bland. But wait too long, and we risk losing the bounty to other wildcrafters. The time to pluck the tunas is in the morning when

Mikey loves harvesting mesquite. We visit stands often and taste the pods, waiting until they're sweet before picking them.

the plant's oxalic acid is low. (Oxalic acid contributes to kidney stones but can be avoided altogether by harvesting at the right time of the day.)

When harvesting prickly pear cactus, we gather only what we can process in a day or two, then go back for more. Wearing welding gloves, Mikey reaches out with a pair of tongs, grabs a fruit from the plant, and twists until it falls into a cardboard box that I hold below.

Never touch the fruit! Its tiny hairlike thorns can take days to find and remove from the skin. At home, we suspend each fruit over a flame with a pair of metal tongs. After the thorns are burned, the fruit is dropped into boiling water to sit for less than a minute. On a wooden cutting board, we split the tuna open and peel back its skin, which we compost. We purée the mush inside, fill ice cube trays with the concentrate, and freeze. When we add prickly pear juice to homemade kombucha, it makes a happy, bright pink carbonated drink that tastes exactly like watermelon Jolly Rancher candy. And it's a natural probiotic to boot!

Other times of the year, we harvest the prickly pear's flat green hand-sized pads and break them down in a bucket mixer filled with water. We strain out the fiber by pouring the mix over a screen and keep the goo inside. The clear jelly makes an antibacterial, water-resistant paint and sealer. The homemade paint that we make with it replaced our need for elastomeric paint, a toxic commercial product that costs about a hundred bucks for a 5-gallon bucket. Prickly pear paint is free and compostable.

Every year Mikey, Sesame, and I visit a sandy spot near Elephant Butte Lake where stands of soapberry trees consider fruiting. They fruited three years ago and not since. "Maybe this year," we say to each other as we head out to check, ready with cloth sacks.

The only berries to be found between fruiting years are at the very tops of the highest branches, amber from age. Soapberries replaced our need for laundry detergent; they're rich in saponin, a chemical compound that foams like soap and has antibacterial properties. About a dozen berries in a muslin sack wash 10 loads of laundry and cost nothing more than a trip to a pretty spot by the lake. When we visit the stands, we take our time, find the lake's edge, and watch a sunset before making our way home.

Since the soapberry stands are near where the yucca grows, we arrive prepared to dig yucca root, which dives deep in sandy ground. Like soapberry, yucca contains saponin. We harvest and dry the root for its soapy attributes and make hair conditioner and a remedy for arthritis. We add hair conditioner and the remedy to our THINGS WE NO LONGER BUY list. When the yucca is in bloom, we pick its iridescent pale sprite petals and add them to salads. Once the yucca flowers bloom, it is hot enough for the rattlesnakes to be out and our visits to these areas near an annual end. After summer, when the snakes are back in their ancient winter dens, we return.

When I forage, I feel as though the cashiers of the world are saying, "You don't have to pay anymore! Everything is free." It's like a waiter tipping *you*. It's like getting in your car and discovering that someone filled your tank while you were asleep. All of nature is a gift. Our common gift.

The fruits of the soapberry tree are quite distinct, with their translucent skin and pebbly surface. They can be used as soap when shaken with water.

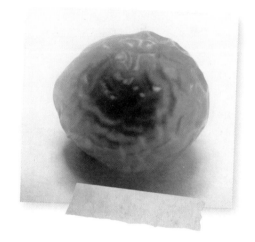

One day I loved the rosemary bush so much that I could not throw away what I pruned. I piled up what I meant to compost as though secretly intending to keep it. A few times I walked by the pile and caught a whiff of the piney smell. I trimmed what I had already cut from it a second time, this time picking the loveliest sprigs, I brought them inside and placed them on the kitchen table, not knowing what for. Later, sitting in front of the pile, I twisted the sprigs together, thinking that I'd never liked wreaths. They seemed old-fashioned in a way that I wasn't. While making this wreath, I thought about knowledge. The knowledge I used to make the rosemary wreath was not acquired in the usual way. I knew how to make a wreath, I reasoned, because I loved the rosemary. I was its student. No one showed me.

When I tore my calf muscle running on a mesa, I limped home and picked comfrey, yarrow, calendula, and yerba mansa from the garden; chopped them semifine; and put the mix in a pot of boiling water on the stove. Then I steeped it for 10 minutes and scooped it onto a small washcloth that I cooled a little before wrapping my leg in it. I thanked the garden, the worms that live in it, the bugs and microbes, the charcoal from the fire pit that I'd mixed into the soil. I noted the carbon before thanking the compost, the heat, the rainwater, and the life of

Over-inspired by The New York Times bestselling book Born to Run, I injured my calf muscle. I made a healing poultice from ingredients in my own garden: comfrey, yarrow, and yerba mansa (as well as a calendula flower just to tell my ripped muscle that it was loved).

this earth. I thanked my friend Catherine for teaching me the recipe and then thanked the sun and thought about how everything alive is a solar cell or a solar converter because everything that lives has taken in the sun's light or heat in one form or another.

Each year before the ant population grows to the size of armies, I offer yoga class in my garden. I remember that there are reasons to know cycles, read signs, and remember nature's timing. I stop holding yoga class at the first sight of lively fine red lines of ants that cross the cement slab like tiny rivers. At least one time each summer I look down and see that I am wearing a red ant sock. I shake it off like a sundancer in a ceremony and then spray on the tincture of the creosote plant that I make each year to calm the feeling of attack.

The first year that we had a garden, Mikey and I grew what probably would have amounted to about 33 cents' worth of cilantro in raised beds that we made out of scraps of wood we plucked from a dumpster. The third year, the garden produced more than we could eat ourselves, and we saved food for winter. Now I look at my garden every morning. I am always surprised by its activity. It shows me that everything alive is in a constant state of change. We added several more beds. The following year we learned to dehydrate, can, and freeze, and sold the eggplant we grew to a health food store two blocks away. Last year I thought that if no other food existed we might survive. Every week this past year I picked fresh flowers for the house and for the houses of friends. For the first time we grew medicine.

Some nights we light a fire in a pit that took me eight hours to dig out. I lined the edge of it with lava rocks that I found while visiting Ted Turner's ranch south of T or C. The wood I burn in the pit comes from the desert just past where the vast expanse begins at the edge of town. We burn mesquite because it smells best. Juniper smells lovely but is harder to come by. We smoke tofu, meat, and fish with the woods we prune from our own fruit trees.

WildCRAFtiNG

NATURE IS ABUNDANT IF YOU KNOW HOW TO LOOK AT IT. LEARN

ABOUT YOUR LOCAL PLANTS, SO YOU CAN FORAGE

FOOD, MEDICINE, AND BUILDING MATERIALS.

INVASIVE SPECIES

THATCHING BRANCHES FROM THE SALT CEDAR
(INVASIVE IN THE SOUTHWEST) MAKES
FENCES AND PATIO WALLS

MULLEIN

AN EXPECTORANT— CLEARS THE LUNGS
REMEDIES SWIMMER'S EAR

PRICKLY PEAR

MAKES A YUMMY PUNCH
MAKES A WATERPROOF SEALANT WHEN ADDED TO
PAINT OR MIXED WITH MORTAR

MESQUITE PODS
GRIND INTO FLOUR
EXTRACT INTO MOLASSES

CREOSOTE
DISINFECTS CUTS, STINGS, AND BITES
ACTS AS AN ANTIFUNGAL

YUCCA
TREATS INFLAMMATION
CONTAINS SAPONIN, GOOD FOR
CLEANING HAIR

HOREHOUND
SOOTHES A SORE THROAT

OCOTILLO
RELIEVES AN UPSET STOMACH

Honeybees that I find in the house hitchhike on my finger to the door, where I encourage them to go outside. I use the honey from their hive to sweeten tea and baked goods; it reduces my susceptibility to pollen allergies. I chew the wax comb as though it's gum. I make lip balm and salve from the wax. One day I will make candles.

In the guest room, a plastic bubbler lodged in the opening of a gallon glass jug of mead releases carbon dioxide (CO_2) into my house, the byproduct of yeast eating the sugar in the honey. As I watch the CO_2 exit the bubbler, I think about it entering my lungs. My respiration transports oxygen to where it is needed in my body. I exhale humidity. I have noticed that the color of our honey is darker when the mesquite trees are in bloom.

I love visiting our bees. Each time I am amazed at their tolerance. I've never been stung, though sometimes I am visiting to steal their honey!

Tuesdays, Beverly the farmer delivers milk to a cooler that we leave by the door. Princess the cow provides the milk. Mikey and I make yogurt and several kinds of cheese with it: mozzarella, Romano, and a Mexican Chihuahua that tastes like cheddar. I say thank you to Princess, to the enzymes, the earth, heat, microorganisms, air, and Beverly.

When my energy is low, I chew sticks from a native plant nicknamed Mormon tea. The nickname came about because the Mormons swore off stimulants yet enjoyed this plant. Turns out, ephedra *is* a stimulant. I sell ephedra tea and tincture in our online store. The local plant does not contain the same alkaloids that are in the illegal Asian variety — the plant that grows in New Mexico is not nearly as strong (though you should still use it with some caution).

When I eat rich foods or too much food, I squirt a dropper full of ocotillo tincture in a cup of water and swig it. The effect is the same as Pepto-Bismol. I harvest the ocotillo plant in the spring, wearing welding gloves that protect my hands from the plant's hard, sharp barbs. I take a stalk or two (never more) from plants growing on private land (with permission). Laws protect the species from being overharvested. I clip the fire-red tops and dry them in paper bags that I attach with clothes-pins to a wire tied between the two corners of my kitchen window. The flaming red tops make a refreshing blush-colored tea. Ocotillo, the sole genus in the *Fouquieriaceae* family, flowers in summer when one is thirsty for tea.

One night I dreamed of potatoes as if I were underground, too. In the morning I got up and harvested the tubers on time. A couple of years later, while I was walking along the Pecos River, a scouring rush plant seemed to tell me that I should notice that it was a remedy for the bladder because it sits by fast-moving water and it grows in the shape of a hollow tube, much like the tubing that leads to the bladder. The same day a mullein plant asked that I notice its furry leaves, similar to the cilia in the lungs. Mullein is an expectorant when it is smoked or steeped in hot water and made into a tea.

I stop writing things down because I understand that the book of nature is the truest book.

I welded together a metal bed frame that was about to be thrown away. I layered soft sheets, blankets, and pillows over a piece of foam so that I can daydream on the bed in the garden. I like to think that Pippi Longstocking is a cousin of mine. My bed can't fly, but it *is* magical. Guests love to sleep in that garden bed, and when they awake in the morning, they have a glow of happiness about them.

At night, under a twinkly purple-black dome, I lie in the garden bed and watch satellites hurry across the sky. They flirt with me half asleep in the soft linen. Before I made the magic bed, I used to blow up an air mattress, put it on the roof, and sleep there with Mikey. In the morning, birds that seemed in the habit of flying a route inches over the roof nearly hit us when we sat up to meet the sunrise.

I go to the highest spot in T or C and stand under the water tower to see the last house in every direction. A fox that lives nearby occasionally makes an appearance. After the last house in every direction begins the vast expanse.

From the 108°F water that comes from a belowground hot spring and is piped into an 8-foot feed tank in my yard, floating and buoyant, I welcome new days and put to rest those that are finished. The sun makes its way over Turtleback Mountain from points south to points north, turning on the equinoxes and solstices. Late summer an impressive band of stars, the Milky Way, tips me off to my cosmic whereabouts. At twilight I see the last shades of blue and green turn purple-black in the same part of the sky that the sun rose in. The moon lifts. "East," I say, confirming the direction. Thin crescent moons seem always to hover in the west. Like a drawn smile, the crescent receives illumination from the sun that can no longer be seen from the side of the planet I am on. I name what I know and promise to know more: the Southern Cross, Orion, the Pleiades, a nebula (a nursery of young stars), another shooting star, the space station. Soon, 30 miles away space flights will take people up to the lower atmosphere. I wonder if I will see them ascend and descend. I smile back at the crescent moon, thinking that I, too, want to catch the light like a bowl, and I consider the ways that I know to ascend and descend. I get a feeling that the universe experiences itself through me, and I yell out loud enough for my neighbors to hear, "*This* is my life."

I go just beyond the boundary of man's world and into the desert to find cures and things I need. The desert is a cure for more than what plants remedy.

A swift white barn owl passes overhead in the night sky without making very much sound. Sure, even-paced movements of strong wings

In summer months I bring my laptop to the garden bed. On hot nights, we sleep in the garden.

Nature Unlocked

displace otherwise still air. I struggle to catch a part of the event and wonder how close I would have to be to feel the sharp cut of air and resulting snap that follows the movement of the giant wings. I close my eyes to see through the eyes of the owl. Movement is of particular interest. I observe a mouse scurry past a cat, unnoticed in the dark in my neighbor's yard, and I wonder if what I am seeing is true.

Almost every night, coyotes squeal to announce a meal, maybe a rabbit, a hundred yards off. Downtown dogs harmonize to the call. Asses living on the only property across the river join in the sound. Sesame's attentive ears stand up, though she stays sitting on the down pillow I made for her out of a blanket my grandmother had lugged to the United States from Russia. I imagine the scene is taking place where the vast expanse begins. Two houses, the river, then the coyote, the mountain, and Jornada del Muerto (dead man's walk), as the natives call the land where Virgin Galactic is building its spaceport.

While I soak in the hot spring in the afternoon, a band of noisy black birds covers all the power lines and rooftops in sight. I try to count the congregations of clattering geese that make enormous Vs in the sky. I have time to try. Everything that I love is free.

The Digital Homestead

Once a new technology rolls over you, if you're not part of the
steamroller, you're part of the road.
— Stewart Brand

Seventeen illuminated laptop screens broke up the darkness of our living room. Thirty-four hands clattering away on the keyboards made a mechanical noise reminiscent of a small factory.

In the kitchen I filled the china cabinet with clean dishes from lunch and noted that it was easier to host this annual meeting of digital homesteaders than it was to have a single houseguest. Somehow the homesteaders made our 1,200-square-foot home feel big enough to hold an army, even when we were huddled hip to hip. Quick to wash a dish, pick up a broom, move a couch, repair an appliance, fix a busted window, or haul wood, homesteaders perform household chores with a familial spirit. The yard is filled with pitched tents and vans parked in front of the old RV park power posts, but on cold nights guests creep into the living room and roll themselves up in a huddle of sleeping bags.

At the kitchen table, video bloggers Jay and Ryan uploaded footage of the previous day's skill-sharing workshop, taught by phycologist Andy Potter. Though Andy's an algae scientist, he had taught a Dutch-oven cooking class that made enough frittata and peach cobbler to keep our bellies full all through the afternoon. Before the other homesteaders could post images of the feast to the web, Ryan announced that her video was online, along with the recipes and techniques.

In the meantime, Asher busied himself by the blender preparing his contribution, a raw-food class on how to make a modified version of key lime pie with a date-nut crust. He began by demonstrating techniques for making lime-infused coconut butter, which he layered with strawberries and pears.

Libby and Tristan took the mystery out of making tempeh (see page 244), a multistep process that combines high protein soybean and a fungus. First they modified a cooler by poking a hole in it for a lightbulb's cord to fit. They installed shelving (oven racks they'd found in a free box by the dumpster). Tristan found parts to complete the fermentation chamber in a scrap heap in the yard and, in no particular rush, he modified the cooler (see page 170).

Cobblers, pies, tempeh: It's not surprising that our annual gathering revolves around food, because our lifestyles do, too. Each evening one

Andy taught us how to cook in a Dutch oven.

third of the group produced the night's dinner for the rest. Those who did not cook cleaned up and restored the kitchen for the next meal.

Gavio produced a dinner game that started with a list of every guest's favorite in-season food: pumpkin, asparagus, pomegranate, basil, okra, and so on. Then he led the group through a contemplative process, to reveal how the seemingly mismatched ingredients could be harmonized into a meal. (Gavio, by the way, was the one who taught us about the importance of kitchen technology. He insisted that without a large food processor and full-strength blender, we were doomed. He was right. Later we added a large food dehydrator, a stovetop smoker, a digital temperature probe, and many other techy tools to our arsenal of kitchen widgets.)

We do more than cook and eat. I taught a welding class, and Mikey led a battery workshop. After Libby and Tristan showed off their home-made rocket stove, Ryan made one out of scrap lying around our yard: a Christmas cookie tin and a soup can. Rocket stoves use combustion and a vertical chimney to burn a remarkably small amount of wood and create an unusually hot flame. Eric gave a presentation on passive homes, and Luke taught basic bike repair out in the yard. We shared and discussed videos about making and building with papercrete. This year everyone was particularly excited to see the leather glove that Eric repaired with a patch he had made out of a kombucha mother that he dried, cut, fit, and sewed where his bike glove had split. Phil was excited about his new laser cutter, a device that rapidly and accurately cuts a variety of materials. He burned Star Trek images into sushi rolls with it. Limor demonstrated a device she had made, a small and inconspicuous remote control. When its button was pressed, it emitted a signal that prevented cell phones from being able to make or receive calls. "A cell phone jammer," she said with a mischievous smile.

We'd first met Jay and Ryan the year we broke ground on our property. A mutual friend had introduced us, knowing they were vlogging (video blogging) about people living alternative lifestyles. They shot a number of short video pieces about Holy Scrap that were picked up by *Make* magazine and received 50,000 views. This buzz connected us to more like-minded people and kicked off our fascination with community development through the Internet. On Jay and Ryan's advice, we started blogging. And when they returned to San Francisco, they pledged themselves to a lifestyle similar to the one we were creating. Within a year they had bought a property in Virginia, renovated it, and begun to grow food, raise bees, and become independent. Between visits we videoconference with them to share our progress, trials, and tribulations.

Our yearly gathering happens because Mikey and I scour the web, looking for people living with similar ideals. We read and comment on each other's blogs. We have in common more than just a lifestyle of making our own goods, living in the waste stream, and growing and preparing food: our homesteads are digital. We blog and have YouTube channels, Flickr accounts, and online stores. We use technology to solve problems. We share ideas and experiences through our blogs and online videoconferences.

Mandy and Ryan appeared at our door with the recumbent bikes that they were riding coast to coast in search of an intentional community to settle in. Someone in town had told them, "You should go meet Wendy and Mikey," and so they did. That night, we watched the videos they had shot at a dozen intentional communities from northern California to Arizona.

In the evenings, a digital projector beamed media from laptops onto our living room wall for more presentations. We soaked in our hot spring and melted s'mores over the fire pit, accompanied by guitars, ukuleles, and things tapped and smashed together to create a clanking rhythm section. I led yoga each morning, and on breaks between skill-sharing workshops our guests scoured local thrift shops for vintage finds. Some packed suitcases with the goods they found and later resold them in eBay stores they maintain to help pay life's expenses.

Between skill-sharing workshops and meals we discussed the irony of our situation. The digital homesteaders gathered at our home use technology, tools, and equipment to create a lifestyle less entangled with money. . . and yet these things require money to obtain. We share a wish to live sustainably on the earth, and yet the production of the things we use comes at a cost to the environment. Our lifestyles are full of contradictions. The PV solar array that Mikey and I installed generates clean power for our home, but its manufacture left a carbon footprint. We use the clean power it produces to run machines made in factories that help us build out of waste materials. Much of what we know about homesteading, growing food, fermenting, composting, repurposing trash, and building began with tutorials found on the Internet. The friendships at our digital homesteader gathering were formed online.

Reconciling these seeming opposites led us to discussions about process, context, and the time we live in. Marginalized, living remotely, without the tie of connectivity offered by technology, we might each be able to reduce our own small footprint more than we already have. But we share a desire to have an effect on more than our individual lives. Technology helps us solve problems and share solutions.

Like Burning Man's temporary city built on goods bought with money produced under the might of capital, our solutions are born out of the context of our time. Black Rock City's gift economy created an example of sharing that impacted people the world over. Swap-O-Rama-Rama is an online community. Cities all over the world could not have used its model for repurposing textile waste if not for global connectivity. Some solutions designed to repair a modern world come with the aid of the technology it spawned.

Mikey and I believe that a world reclaimed by individual makers will be a better one than the world run by corporations because individual makers are not commodified. Corporations are bound by law to make decisions that produce the greatest profit for their shareholders. Profit-driven corporations disperse decision making across departments and formulize the process so that decisions with destructive outcomes are made by no single person. In corporations you'll find people saying things like *I just file the paperwork, I only check the pipe fittings, I install the computer systems, I just run the wiring, I only manage the budget,* and *My only job is purchasing the hardware.* Ask the same individuals if they would dump toxic waste into a river and they'll likely say no. But as employees of a corporation that dumps toxic waste into a river, they all play a tiny part even if they don't realize it.

In contrast, individual makers are directly connected to outcomes. Free of the mandate of profit, they make decisions differently. Individuals have the luxury of considering *life.* A fundamental question we must ask is, *Who has the power to make decisions that impact us all?*

People alive today are tasked with transforming something already built, failing, and destructive into something better. We are past the moment in which fretting over each plastic bag matters. We don't have the hundred years that is needed for consumer behavior to add up to having an impact. Fretting over the plastic bag distracts us from the abuses of those who manufactured the bag. Industrial waste, the burning of fossil fuels, and the resources consumed by corporations, supported by governments, and driven by capital, outweigh individual consumer behavior immeasurably. Bill McKibben reported in a July 2012 article in *Rolling Stone* that the U.S. Chamber of Commerce, after giving 90 percent of its political cash to the Republican Party in 2010, filed a brief with the Environmental Protection Agency urging it not to regulate carbon. In response to the question *What if the scientists turn out to be right?* a Chamber representative said, "Populations can acclimatize to warmer climates via a range of behavioral, physiological and technological adaptations." The U.S. Chamber suggests that in Darwinian fashion humanity adapt to a world whose signature is continual destruction. "Thanks to the size of its bankroll, the fossil-fuel industry has far more free will than the rest of us," McKibben concluded. Of corporations invested in hydrocarbons, such as Shell, BP, Exxon, Chevron, and Peabody, he wrote, "They hold the power to change the physics and chemistry of our planet, and they're planning to use it." In the same article, he quotes Naomi Klein: "Lots of companies do rotten things in the course of their business — pay terrible wages, make people work in sweatshops — and we pressure them to change those practices. . . . For the fossil-fuel industry, wrecking the planet is their business model. It's what they do." Vananda Shiva, author of *Stolen Harvest*, describes the push/pull of industry and nature by saying, "Nature shrinks as capital grows." She, too, believes that the "abuse of the earth *is* the ecological crisis."

As creatures of this earth we share in the right to use and protect our common treasures: water, air, and soil are yours to use (or not) to make things better. Individuals make better decisions than corporations. You can consider more than profit. You can consider context, balance, harmony, and life. When you make decisions wisely, things get better all the time.

The Least Useful Most Fun Thing

To understand pleasure is not to deny it.
— Krishnamurti

Not all of our techy projects were designed for practical purposes. While our guests napped and milled about between workshops, Mikey fired up a plasma cutter in our sun-baked yard. He tinkered with a scrap piece of 4-inch square by 6-foot metal tubing that he planned to use to shoot fireballs from a trampoline. He first debuted the strange toy at Fiesta, an annual townwide event featuring a quintessential small-town parade of Shriners driving midget cars in fast-spinning circles, a proud sheriff's posse on horseback, and lots of floats. T or C's annual Fiesta weekend also featured a rodeo, a karaoke contest, and quirky games like the racing of rubber duckies down the Rio Grande. Thanks to Mikey, Fiesta also included one fire trampoline.

The trampoline (found in a dumpster) appeared to be perfectly normal until someone jumped on it and activated an EZ1 ultrasonic sensor below that read the distance between the stretched canvas and the ground. This caused a solenoid valve to release an appropriately sized spurt of gas from the top of a nearby metal stand with a lit wick at its tip. An LCD screen connected to the device provided data, such as the depth of jump based on the height of the trampoline and the amount of propane expected to be released. Our homesteader guests enjoyed a night of competing to produce the largest flame while bouncing up and down on the trampoline in our yard.

Like the Brooks Brothers suit Mikey had hacked into a pair of illuminated pinstripe pants back in New York, the trampoline was a protest to a world left behind, a world fixated on the acquisition of wealth. He described it as "the least useful, most fun thing I could think of making." Wall Street was fast fading from view.

We planned to reconfigure the device later by turning it into a flaming doorbell. We reasoned that would be more practical. To transform it we needed only to swap the LCD screen for an old surveillance camera, to take a snapshot of the person who rang the doorbell, thus capturing their response to the surprise fire display. We planned to have the device e-mail us the photo so that we would know who was at the door. Sometimes geekery is not efficient or logical, though in this case, you must admit, it did have a practical, even if mischievous, application.

Mikey's controls for the fire trampoline include one LCD screen that shows the jumper in action and one that gives the trampoline's start height, the jumper height, and the difference between them. The device also rates the jump with a score.

The Least Useful Most Fun Thing

165

A Cottage Industry

I don't want to sell anything, buy anything, or process anything
as a career. I don't want to sell anything bought or processed,
or buy anything sold or processed, or process anything sold,
bought, or processed, or repair anything sold, bought, or
processed.

— LLOYD DOBLER, PLAYED BY JOHN CUSACK, IN *Say Anything*

Mikey and I delighted in the autonomous zone that small-town life offered us far and away from corporate logos and heavy commerce, but this life also offered no clear way to earn even the little income our lifestyle still demanded. When we were finished building our homestead's infrastructure — garden beds, papercrete domes, irrigation systems, shade, and our PV solar system — we turned our attention to technology to help us devise a way to earn money. Still asking ourselves, *Is there a way to live that does not require money?* and *Can we discover it before we run out?*, we looked for a way to earn income that did not compromise our new lifestyle. Shopkeepers in town waited for customers to appear while carrying huge overheads and paying for utilities. We knew there had to be a better way. As homesteaders, we spend our time providing for our needs: making cheese, building, tending to gardens, and making medicines. These activities reduce our cost of living by more than five times. Our financial solution had to complement our homesteading lifestyle.

In 2010 we started a web-based cottage industry, the Holy Scrap Store, with the idea that we would make a little extra of the things that we made for ourselves and offer it to others. I often thought of Helen and Scott Nearing; part of their income came from harvesting and selling maple syrup and maple sugar they made from sap tapped from trees on their Vermont farm. We took what was natural and particular to where we lived and turned it into economy.

The Chihuahuan desert where we live is host to an unusual bounty of medicinal plants unique to its altitude and climate. By wildcrafting plants from the desert and relying on what we made out of them to help support us, we entered into a new relationship with nature and recognized our responsibility. We harvested where life was abundant, never taking more than was necessary, never cutting more than 20 percent from any one plant, and moving about from year to year, giving stands time to recuperate.

Not much about our lifestyle really changed by having a cottage industry; we just produced a little more than we needed and posted it to the store. The teas that we favored in our home, made from local plants mixed with plants from our garden, we offered as medicinal blends. If I made lip balm or salve from the wax produced by the beehive in the garden, I made a little extra and put it in the store. I enjoyed the way that running the store diversified my skills and revived the graphic design skills that I'd picked up in college and had let go rusty. I designed product labels, merchandising materials, and the store's site with great interest.

It was at one of our annual homestead gatherings that Mikey decided to design electronic gadgets. Three hardware developer homesteaders standing shoulder to shoulder in the kitchen cringed, watching Libby struggle with a reptile timer to aid in the making of tempeh. Frustrated by the timer's poor functionality and realizing that the right widget could offer a great deal to the process, Mikey said, "I can do better than this," and set out to design a temperature controller to solve dozens of problems related to producing and processing food.

First he used his temperature controller to transform our home energy use. We reduced the power consumption of our home's largest energy sucker, our refrigerator, by replacing it with a chest freezer that we acquired for $50 at a garage sale. We turned the freezer into a refrigerator by plugging it into the temperature controller and setting the temperature. The conversion reduced our home's power draw for refrigeration by 10 times by freeing up a big dose of the power produced by our PV solar system.

After the refrigerator conversion, we used the gadget that Mikey named Yet Another Temperature Controller (YATC) to make a fermentation chamber out of a small, nonworking wine refrigerator that a friend was throwing away. We plumbed the fridge with a light socket and bulb for heat, plugged it into YATC, and set the temperature to match our use, whether we were making tempeh, letting bread dough rise, or making yogurt. The temperature controller also transformed a simple $20 slow cooker into a sous vide device, which we also use to separate honey from wax and slow-cook meat and tough veggies. Able to regulate any device plugged into it to run hotter or colder, the temperature controller Mikey designed gives precision control to a hot plate, enabling it to hold specific temperatures for specialized uses such as chocolate-making. The temperature controller gave us back time, reduced our labor, and helped us achieve the goal of keeping our food living, unpasteurized, and enzymatically active. Our cheeses and honey meet the qualification of raw by having never been heated beyond the threshold in which microorganisms live.

In keeping with the motto *Make extra of the things we use*, we added the temperature controller to the Holy Scrap Store. Embracing the open-source ethic, keeping knowledge free and sharing it, Mikey also posted the source code and hardware designs for the device's circuit board to the web. Then he made YATC available both in finished and kit form, for those who wished to make the device themselves. As YATC began to sell, he looked for other homesteading problems to solve with technology.

With the glee of a 12-year-old graduate of Willy Wonka University, Mikey went on to build a device that reads and responds to the moisture level in the earth by turning on our irrigation system when the soil is dry. While expensive store-bought gadgets triggered by timers water gardens during rainstorms, Mikey's device releases precious desert water only when it is actually needed.

When he found himself spending too much time tracking the location of clogs in Chance's fuel lines, he designed the Greasy Mon, a device that reads heat levels at various points along the fuel lines. The Greasy Mon indicated clogged fuel lines by showing where the temperature increased and decreased, thus pointing to blocks in the line.

When we wanted to sprout seeds and grow plants indoors, he designed an LED-based indoor grow light that reduced the light spectrum to the colors plants most need. He oscillated the LEDs at a rate unobservable to the human eye and to plants, and reduced the power draw.

Recognizing the important role batteries play in off-grid life and aware of the toxic effect of batteries in landfills, Mikey next made a device for restoring dead batteries. His soap dish battery desulfator that he calls Power in My Pocket (PIMP) revives free junk batteries headed for the landfill. The battery desulfator works by emitting a high frequency pitch to a battery; the sound breaks up the crystallization inside and brings back the battery's vitality. Fewer new batteries would be purchased, toxic chemicals reduced, minerals left in the earth.

Making homebuilt electronics had us buying premade parts that we sourced from outside suppliers. At first Mikey designed the circuit boards at home and sent them out to be manufactured. He used premade casings purchased from vendors to house the finished products. Wanting to do more of the work ourselves, he purchased a computer numeric control (CNC) (see page 259). When the CNC machine arrived, he spent several days assembling the unit (he bought it in kit form) and several months mastering and perfecting its use. It required calibration and the learning of a host of new software. He reflected that having a job would have lengthened his learning curve and pushed back

HACKING APPLI-ANCES

with YATC

The open-source movement has welcomed everyone into the world of electronics. For example, Mikey made YATC (yet another temperature controller) so that we can make things warm/hot/cool/cold with just about any device.

turn a...

camping cooler into a fermenter for making kimchi, tempeh, yogurt and rising bread dough.

hot plate into a cooker for making cheese, candy, syrup, and molasses.

crock pot into a sous vide for slow-cooking vacuum-sealed food and for separating honey and wax.

dorm fridge into a wine or cheese refrigerator.

chest freezer into a refrigerator (reduce power consumption by 10x).

keep unnecessary food items out.

the goal of self-sufficiency. Today we home-manufacture many of his devices' parts and packaging, including the circuit boards.

As our cottage industry picked up speed I recognized a familiar invitation at our door. We were being invited to upscale. Money was making its round, and I imagined the familiar goblins saying, "How 'bout now? Betcha could use a little extra cash." Ten years into my pledge, I was prepared for the temptation.

Many times throughout my life my father asked me, usually when I picked up a new interest, "Can you make *real* money doing that?" I've explained our credo to my mom, but still each time Mikey makes a new gadget she asks, "Is he going to patent it?" Mikey would not patent his widgets, and we would not choose to upscale.

It seems natural that each new generation is tasked with seeking a remedy for the wounds of those that came before. My parents were born during the Great Depression.

"Ma! We have enough," I tell her. She smiles and nods in agreement, as if to say she simply forgot.

While considering the decision to expand our cottage industry, Mikey checked in with friends of ours who were running a successful home manufacturing business and had expanded theirs. They complained about having tons of money but no time. They were stressed out. They described larger and larger debt, bigger stakes, greater risk, more people to manage, more reasons not to sleep, more stress, and more hours spent working.

To tease out some of the issues related to the decisions we faced, we split a laptop screen to view two blank pages and started two lists (see pages 174–5).

We decided to let our cottage industry reach a ceiling defined by our being able to handle all its aspects ourselves, from our 1-acre homestead. The only help we would take on would come in the form of child labor. Well, sort of. Mikey tutors friends' children on how to work with electricity and electronics. Some sessions resulted in built gadgets. We chose not to patent, outsource, promote, or seek channels of distribution and not to engage in activities that led to more people driving to work, more paper moved, insurance bought, lawyers engaged, sunsets missed, and sleep lost. We chose time over money: by limiting our own growth I could still teach yoga, build the giant metal flower I imagined mounted to the signpost in front of our property, and live the life we had worked hard to create. We would continue to make cheese, build things, and take Sesame on long walks along the Rio Grande. Mikey

Working with Mikey has helped Ashe know that in the future he will become an engineer. Mikey says he has surgeon's hands.

UPSCALE

Wealth

Less time: more store-bought and lower-quality goods

Stress: deadlines, paperwork, and activity of business

Need for specialists like lawyers and accountants

Monotony: life narrowed, less diverse experience of life, specialization. Disproportionate amount of time spent on a single thing.

Requires survival mentality: selling, deal-making, competition, negotiations, strategizing to get the best of a situation for personal gain, competing. "Every man for himself" mentality.

Time spent unenjoyably: red tape, liability, managing regulations. More time on phones and computers indoors, less time in nature.

More acculturated knowledge. Less independence.

Managing and employing other people. Artificial relationships.

Business risk is tied to forces outside our control: worry, risk, more to lose.

VOLUNTARILY LIMITED GROWTH

Abundance

Grow and prepare healthy fresh food; make hand-made, high-quality goods

Slower pace: moderate time spent on paperwork and working with artificial systems

Simplicity: Understand and manage all aspects of our lives ourselves

Maintain a diversity of interests and skills. Continue to grow.

A lifestyle of generosity and sharing, free of the constraints of profit. Can make decisions based on preserving life rather than supporting industry. Relationships are natural and not contrived for mutual gain.

Time spent enjoying life, traveling, playing. Time spent in nature and outdoors.

More natural knowledge about life: plants, planet, people, and the common sense. Independence.

Participate in community and friendships rather than artificial relationships based on financial structures. Don't have to be anyone's employer or boss.

Less worry and risk: Life is not subject to swings of market.

would be free to develop new skill sets, make things for pleasure's sake, help friends with their technical problems, and find solutions, making life a little better all the time. We chose to preserve the sensuous life of growing, processing, cooking, and eating food; soaking in the hot springs; daydreaming on the iron bed in the garden; and counting birds in the sky.

Mikey and I decided that if our cottage industry store failed or faded, if something in the world changed and made it irrelevant, we would simply find something else to do.

wisdom

The essence of milk is butter, the essence of the flower is honey,
the essence of grapes is wine, and the essence of life is wisdom.
Wisdom is not necessarily a knowledge of names and forms;
wisdom is the sum total of that knowledge which one gains both
from within and without.

— HAZRAT INAYAT KHAN

While writing this book, many times I noticed that the knowledge I
have to share was not passed down to me through the cultural milieu,
even though many of the problems that Mikey and I went about solving
are as old as humanity. The knowledge I gathered to fulfill the pledges I
made was pieced together from the Internet, people I found living outside the margins of mainstream culture, hard-to-find and out-of-print
books, trial and error, and contemplative practice. I wondered why my
formal education failed to pass on fundamental knowledge about how
to live. What I felt missing was my relatedness to my species, my relationship to life and how to live within it, essential knowledge. This kind
of knowledge, amassed across the arc of time, seems to have dropped
off in the last hundred years. I felt like I was an odd fit in the world. My
upbringing in the suburbs of Long Island and adult life in the city did
not help me find the knowledge I craved. Throughout my education I
had learned how civilization worked, but no one taught me how to live
on the earth.

As Douglas Rushkoff points out in *Life Inc.*, "The techniques for
proper breastfeeding used to be passed down from mother to daughter,
but now there is a market for lactation consultants. As a result, one of the
most intimate human functions has become commodified." For at least

a half-century people have learned about media, brands, and commerce. Not how they work, but how to work them. They learned about systems within systems: coupons, warranties, return policies, credit cards, and things related to the economy. As part of the first generation to witness the whole world for sale, fully commodified, and nature under genuine duress, we are finding that the knowledge relied on by previous generations cannot solve the problems that new generations face.

All my life I have observed a nervous and fearful humanity. I wonder what this condition tells us about the time we live in. Over half a century ago, journalist Edward R. Murrow said,

> *There is a creeping fear of doubt, doubt of what we have been taught, of the validity of so many things we had long since taken for granted to be durable and unchanging. It has become more difficult than ever to distinguish black from white, good from evil, right from wrong.*

I wonder if people are afraid because they know that they don't understand the *real* world? Acculturated knowledge is shallow, and the landscape of commerce is not necessarily logical, fair, reliable, sensible, or just. The footing is unsteady.

When we know that we are safe with ourselves we feel calm and happy. We are naturally wired with a need to know that we are qualified to care for ourselves. The suspicion and fear I see tell me that the knowledge we carry is not the right kind; it is not good enough. Many of us do not trust ourselves with ourselves.

I've noticed that many in the generations who welcomed in the commodified world rely on a mysterious *they* for information about how to live. "*They* say ginkgo is no longer good but B_{12} is essential." "*They* say we should spend twenty minutes a day in the sun with no sunblock." I hear the snake-oil salesmen saying, "Hurry hurry!" while waving bottles of potions in the air. In this atmosphere people are left to guess about the motives of the mysterious *they* and hope that their best interests are somehow being served. In a society based on capital, the motives should be well understood. If our culture has no genuine source of wisdom, people have no choice but to be scared. Without wisdom we are marooned.

Since we are part of the natural world, civilization's acculturated knowledge is not our own. We cannot intuit it. People are meant to intuit our world because essentially we are not other than the world. It would be silly to think we cannot know ourselves. That would be like starving to death because we failed to notice that we were hungry. This is not how nature works. Nature is logical; it makes perfect sense. It is *the* common sense. Nature's rules are reliable.

For a world that cannot be intuited and is difficult to understand, we have created a variety of interpreters: lawyers, accountants, and highly specialized people who interpret civilization's complex code. Since civilization does not come naturally to people, this causes every step in life to contain the weight of the world. With no natural system to decipher or intuit with, our nervous system goes ballistic. Welcome nervousness, fear, dis-ease.

I have learned that knowledge is not obtained exclusively with our brains; it is gained through our hearts and by reconnecting to life, a source of wisdom. Makers of things are in a position to understand and change the world. Buyers of things need only know where to find what they want and have the money to pay for what they're buying: acculturated knowledge. But makers of things know what things are made of, how they work, where they come from, what their real cost is, and how to fix them. Makers are connected to the world because everything that is made comes from the world. In my pursuit of a decommodified life, I came to believe that when all of life is for sale, it is a revolutionary act to become a maker of things.

James Fadiman said, "Whatever we wish to know well, we must love." All the knowledge that I acquired started out with love, a desire

to connect to the thing I wished to know. In the form of desire — a spark of creativity, interest, and curiosity — I applied my attention to problems and in return gained insight.

The inverse of what Fadiman said is equally true: we cannot truly love what we do not know. Every day I see human beings separate themselves through branding, cues read as signs that we are not related. Connection to life includes connection to people. This is why whatever is learned must immediately be shared so that *we* can survive and enjoy life. When curiosity connected me to the world, my desire transformed and became communication, communion, and empathy. The magic bridge between people and the things of the world, is material and emotional. Once connected to the world, I felt accountable to it. This is when I caught a glimpse of what value really is. *Value is responsibility.*

During the decade that passed since making the first of many pledges, I thought long and hard about objects. I wondered why we worked hard to obtain things that we immediately threw away. I noticed that shame was embedded in our creations: sweat labor, pollution, the diminishing of life, our lives. I found that today's manufactured objects point to where value is absent, and so I decided to make things that I value. I stopped buying mimics of what I already owned, nature transformed by machines and made into products, things that I paid for with the cost of life. Instead I made my goods out of trash and natural materials because I learned that it is not the *thing* that has value, but the life that made the thing and the life respected in the process. Then I put the things I made in a world that I learned to treasure by reconnecting to it. The best of myself, projects like Swap-O-Rama-Rama, I turned into gifts because only the gift has the force needed to move mountains. No longer *other*, the life of the world in all its forms became my own life, a life I wished to preserve.

I have always imagined wisdom as something old, savored, experienced, tested, proven, and worn. At first I thought of it as something that cannot be lost, since wisdom is mainly stored in people. But wisdom *can* be lost: we lose it when we stop participating in life. This is what happened when our culture became commodified. We traded presence (the living) for representation (a lifeless mimic).

Lived knowledge adapts and revivifies, remains always fresh, and is renewed by each generation's creativity, by makers. Indigenous cultures know this. They transfer wisdom from person to person, from one generation to the next. Crafted by countless faces and through all times, each generation applies the wisdom given to them to their own lives. They make wisdom a living thing, reshape it by fitting it to a new time, and translate it to prepare it for who comes next. I think this shows us that knowledge has to be lived in an unbroken chain — otherwise it no longer applies to the problems of the day; it becomes extinct.

If just a couple of generations choose not to use the knowledge that was passed down to them, a few centuries later people scratch their heads because they can barely remember it or find it no longer applies. They say, "Wisdom is lost," and throw their arms in the air in frustration. People are doing this today.

Sometimes I imagine people of the future gathered together reflecting on our culture and this time. We will be remembered as the people who consumed abundant fuel and energy in the flash of a hundred years. I imagine future people holding one of our trinkets, something they found in an archeological dig, maybe a Hello Kitty key chain. They look at each other and say, "They spent it on gum."

As I watch monetary systems crash and life shift and move like lava, I am not afraid because I know that what is dying never contained life. "Life lives," the Sufis say. *We* are life; in each age humans, bees, microorganisms, and blades of grass live. The Sufis also say that only death dies. I know that our economic system, which is dying today, never contained life.

Pruning a rosemary bush, I became intoxicated by its scent and made my first wreath. I needed neither the word "wreath" nor its history to know how. Love of the scent led me.

When I found myself throwing my hands up in the air and went out looking for knowledge, I found it from within and without. I combined what I was able to gather from this world, tidbits of wisdom that trickled down in spite of being dismissed as no longer relevant, with what could be intuited through a connection to life, to nature.

Now I know that essential knowledge needs no liaison, university, license, or permit. It is available to every one of us in every moment, and it is free. The best of the wisdom that was left to us points back to the truest book, of which we are a part. Nature is the truest book.

To read the book we need only tune ourselves to it, an innate skill given to all that lives. It is fundamentally true that we are a part of nature, that everything alive is; we can't help it. When we connect to nature through our senses and imaginations, no necessary thing is secret. Nature has no secrets, only gifts.

We once knew how to connect, and clues of it are in our languages. The world *religion* has a Latin root that means "reconnect"; the root of the word *universe* is "toward one"; *nirvana* means "no difference." The African word *ubuntu* as it was translated by Leymah Gbowee means "I am what I am because of who we all are." "You can't be human all by yourself," said Archbishop Desmond Tutu.

My reward for reconnecting is that I feel free and related to something imperishable: life. Not the life of a single thing or a creature named Wendy but *the* life. When civilization prompts me to be specialized, when someone asks Wendy, "What do you do?" I used to answer, "I'm in marketing." Today I answer differently. I say what I think the person asking the question will understand. Sometimes I say things like "I teach yoga," "I produce events," "I am a conceptual artist, a green builder." I hope for the day when the real answer will be understood: "I do what needs to be done." That's all any of us has to do. Buckminster Fuller knew this when he said,

> The things to do are: the things that need doing, that you see need to be done, and that no one else seems to see need to be done. Then you will conceive your own way of doing that which needs to be done — that no one else has told you to do or how to do it. This will bring out the real you that often gets buried inside a character that has acquired a superficial array of behaviors induced or imposed by others on the individual.

Today the little plastic troll I bought in Topanga Canyon on my cross-country drive sits on my bedroom dresser. She reminds me where I have been and where I have arrived and all that happened along the way. She reminds me that I once did not feel safe with myself. Today, I know that intuition can be relied on because I remember how I acquired it. The philosopher's stone is in the heart of the sincere, the only safe place for a thing of value to be stored. The magic keys to obtain a working heart are readily available and found in nature. I also learned that to discover any true thing we must first come out to meet it; as Fadiman said, we must love that which we wish to know.

Nature makes no duplicates. Though everything alive contains nature's code, DNA, everything alive is also differentiated; no two things are entirely alike; each contains its own share of the common sense. You have something to offer this world that no other can. Without your participation, life is incomplete. Something is missing.

Our invitation is to play, to love the life of this world, and to listen to what it says with all the desire we can muster. We don't read life or think life; these are techniques of acculturated knowledge. Tools left behind, knowledge carried person to person, and wisdom captured in books, though meant to guide us, can only take us so far. Life is lived. Sensory experience is our language with the rest of life. When we come out to meet the life of this world, we can make wisdom living again and revive the common sense. My generation can pass something on to those who come after us. We can tell the people who come next that we are creators. The pledges I made and everything that followed them led me to see the task of the time that I live in. We are here to revive the soul of this world. And we already have all the tools we need to do it.

part III

LIFE

LAB

Mad skills

When the whole world is for sale, the maker of things is the revolutionary of the age.

— THE HOLY SCRAP CREDO

A postconsumer life requires what Mikey and I call *mad skills*. When you set out to decommodify your life, you don't need to have mad skills, but you do need to *acquire* them if you are going to be successful. Once you have mad skills, you will be able to make and have things that are not available in stores. Things money can't buy. With mad skills, most things can be repaired without the help of others. The best way to acquire mad skills is to make things, break things, and take things apart. Experiment. Play and rediscover the world.

Start projects. Sometimes this might seem a little scary. Consider what Chris Hackett said: *Fear is never boring.*

Start even if you don't how. Perfection is an illusion. Do not aim for it. If it doesn't work out, you can get someone to fix it later.

When you discover a skill you want to have, search for information about it on the web. You might find a tutorial that demonstrates the skill being used: Instructables, Hack a Day, Adafruit, Flickr, YouTube, and technique-oriented media such as *Make* magazine or *Craft* are good sources for step-by-step instructions about how to make and fix things. Invite others to demonstrate their skills to you in person. Offer to make them lunch or gift them appropriately. You might invite them to peruse your junk pile. Tinkerers love junk. Offering them something from your junk stash is perfectly fine etiquette in the world of makers of things.

Repairs and hacks differ from projects started from scratch. Repairs and hacks need only that you take something apart, remove an item's body or case, and get into the guts of a thing like an electronic gadget or a broken car. New projects benefit from a sketch of what you plan to do, a guess at the expected measurements, and a list of tools and materials you think you will need.

The start of any project can be frustrating. Without experience, systems, procedures, and tools, beginnings can be messy and require multiple trips to the store (or the trash) for things you did not anticipate needing. This is especially true of plumbing projects. Start plumbing projects when you know that the stores that sell plumbing supplies are open.

When starting a project, expect things to go wrong; know that you will refine and create systems as you gain experience. A stack of books

The recipe for this batch of umber papercrete mortar failed. It peeled weeks after we applied it. We blogged about it so others could learn from our mistake.

cannot replace hands-on experience. Keep in mind that understanding follows experience and causes knowledge to grow exponentially.

When beginning a project, consider documenting the process for the benefit of others. Take a before photo and note your activities in stages so that you can share your experience. Failed attempts, when shared, are valuable: they prevent others from making the same mistake. Photo documentation and detailed notes can be helpful for you, too, especially for repairing something that is easy to take apart and hard to put back together.

Once you have acquired a mad skill, consider how to share your new knowledge. Invite friends over and show them what you know. Mikey and I regularly host parties that demonstrate things like making 5 gallons of wine; preparing kombucha brew; making tempeh, tinctures, and biofuel; and cutting a 50-gallon metal drum into a fire barrel. People love skill-sharing parties, especially those that revolve around food.

Do for the doing. As consumers we are familiar with the buying part of being makers. Do you remember starting a new school year and thinking that the pristine notebook you bought would inspire perfect penmanship? A few scribbles later that idea was down the tubes. How about the inspiration you felt starting a new hobby? Many hobbies end minutes after the supplies are purchased. Coming out of consumer culture requires breaking the habit of acquiring and instead holding our focus on the making of the thing. Try out the mantra *Do for the doing.*

Start by making what you buy. Start small and consider what you buy and what you might be able to make yourself. Write down the savings produced by making what you once bought, and tally the savings as the lists grow. A list will help you choose projects to prioritize. On the next page, you'll find our still-growing list. This year I hope to learn to make liquid soap and shampoo.

WHAT WE NO LONGER BUY

BIG STUFF
- Fuel (two electric vehicles powered by on-site PV solar system and two biodiesel vehicles that burn homemade fuel)
- Power (PV solar 2-kilowatt system)
- Hot water for bathing (hot spring on our property; we don't have a hot water heater)
- Insulation (homemade papercrete)
- Furniture and home décor (garbage picked and refurbished or made from scrap)

HOUSEHOLD
- Vinegar (made from kombucha)
- Glass cleaner (vinegar from kombucha + water)
- Wax for salve and candles (from our on-site beehive)
- Sponges (loofah plant grown in our garden)
- Most clothing (swaps)
- Laundry detergent (wildcrafted soapberries used instead of detergent)
- Gifts (handmade and homegrown)
- Flowers (garden)

COSMETICS AND MEDICINES
- Lip balm (wax from beehive, plants harvested, and herbal oils made)
- Salve, skin moisturizer (wax from beehive, plants harvested, and herbal oils made and mixed)
- Hair conditioner (vinegar + plant-based teas)
- Soap (homemade)
- Toothpaste (baking powder + peppermint essential oil + Dr. Bronner's soap)
- Haircuts

FOOD

- Plant protein (tempeh, mushrooms)
- Flour-based foods (homemade breads, pancakes/muffins, pastas, baked sweets, phyllo dough, and so forth)
- Cheese and yogurt (made from raw local cow's milk)
- Sweetener (honey from bees)
- Tomato sauce (garden)
- Jams (garden)
- Pesto (garden)
- Vegetable stock (garden)
- Veggies and greens (garden)
- Culinary herbs (garden)
- Medicinal herbs (garden and wildcrafted)
- Woods for smoking foods (foraged)

BEVERAGES

- Wine (kits)
- Mead (from beehive's honey)
- Smoothies (fruit and yogurt from local raw cow's milk)
- Roasted coffee (green coffee beans roasted in a garage sale popcorn maker)
- Teas (local and homegrown plants)
- Fruit drinks (homegrown and local fruits)
- Carbonated beverages (yeast-activated and kombucha)

LANDSCAPE

- Compost (from our kitchen scraps)
- Fertilizer (free camel poo from Stanley the camel)
- Mulch (free from the city)
- Wood for building (scrap from trash)
- Dormant oil, a natural pesticide (homemade from WVO + baking soda + hydrogen peroxide + tea tree oil)
- Garden trellis for climbing plants (thrown-away bed frames)

Use waste. We live amid the largest surplus ever to exist. And we are in the middle of an environmental crisis. Since all new resources come at a cost to life, we ought to show examples of good etiquette by choosing waste rather than demanding that new materials be harvested for our consumption. Choosing waste is the polite thing to do. Waste is a low-cost or free material that encourages taking risks, which is great for learning and developing building skills. You have *nothing to lose*. Using waste is guilt-free. Using waste extends the life of raw materials that have already been harvested. It's hard to know the real cost of a new item — consider objectionable labor practices, pollution, fossil fuels burned in production and transportation — but it's clear that using anything a bit longer is better for the life of our planet.

Check in with your sanitation department to find out what reuse materials are available. Often recycling centers collect but do not recycle materials. These materials can be obtained for free. If you are new to a rural area or small town, befriending a local who knows the ins and outs of available materials may prove very helpful.

Seek simple, unabstracted natural materials such as cotton, wool, linen, hemp, stone, wood, and metal. Natural, simple materials have not been severely processed and are often compostable. I have composted entire cotton sheet sets and clothing made with natural fibers by using them to line garden beds. Unabstracted materials have a lower cost to the environment, are more durable, and are more easily repurposed. Even when these goods have been made into something, they remain raw materials. In this way they are inherently more valuable.

Go a step further by learning about the raw materials that are natural to your area. Favor natural, local materials for building and making things. Find out about how the native population used local resources. Seeking out such resources may very well have the added benefit of getting you to visit beautiful places.

Mikey and I discovered that the gooey middle of New Mexico's prickly pear cactus had been used by Native Americans to make a waterproof, antibacterial additive for mortar and paint. When we started to use the cactus goo ourselves, we saved hundreds of dollars and replaced elastomeric paint with something we make ourselves from a locally abundant plant.

Invasive species present a good place to look for free materials. Salt cedar, a tree that was brought to the United States from Asia, consumes too much water to be welcome in the Southwest. This makes it a resource whose harvesting has no negative consequences. We harvest it in the desert and use the wood for thatching outdoor projects, reinforcement grids inside papercrete slabs (for tensile strength), and firewood.

Following what the natives in our area once did, we chopped up prickly pear cactus pads with a bucket mixer to get the goo inside, and then mixed it with paper, cement, and umber to make a water-resistant coating.

Consider everything you buy your responsibility to deal with — including the packaging. Find a new owner for what you acquire and no longer want, make something out of your waste, or (better yet) don't buy what will later be unnecessary.

Part of this responsibility is to know where your waste goes. It's not good enough that waste be taken away. You may be surprised to learn where it all ends up. Recycling has a carbon footprint, too.

Buy goods from people rather than from corporations. People-made goods have more inherent value than machine-made goods.

If you must buy new goods, hold companies responsible for the products they produce. Follow up on warranties to prevent excess materials from going to landfills and to encourage better manufacturing practices.

Buy used goods. Most things can be found secondhand, on eBay, or in the trash. Chemicals used in industrial manufacturing processes dissipate over time (they off-gas), making used goods less toxic. Once I know what I want, it appears in the waste stream in no time at all. I specify details like materials and color, and my finds have matched what I imagined.

The goods we own and mingle with in our daily lives are a reflection of us. Buying new goods is no crime, but by considering what we buy, we create the conditions that allow us to appreciate what we own. Flimsy goods that produce waste and pollution come with resentment. Goods, used or new, become special when we value them. Consider the process by which things were made, their durability and longevity, their cost to life.

Here's a desk I found for $20. It is solid wood and has good lines, so I sanded it down and refinished it with linseed oil.

I found this wire chair from the 1970s in the trash and gave it a fresh coat of paint. I reupholstered the cushions in sturdy shade cloth.

Fix what breaks. Fixing things is a way to explore materials and find out how things work.

If you can't fix it or open it, you don't own it.

— MR. JALOPY, A WEST COAST MAKER

Consider this motto when acquiring goods that may be designed with planned obsolescence in mind (or at the very least, to prevent opening and tinkering). If you try to fix something and fail, you will still have gained experience and some spare parts.

Consider context. Living a decommodified life in a commodified world presents compromises. Our world runs on batteries, one of the most toxic substances in landfills. Mikey created a battery desulfator that revives batteries and extends their life, thus reducing what goes to landfill. But the parts Mikey uses to build his desulfators are manufactured and come at a cost to the environment. We use manufactured appliances like sewing machines and welders to build and make things out of waste. We use computers to learn how to live more sustainably and share what we know.

To reduce the impact of the waste created by these modern aids, rely on the waste stream. Purchase used computers a couple of generations out of date and sell the ones you've been using; drive older cars, fix them yourself, and power them on alternative homemade fuels; use gadgets and tools that are refurbished, and fix them when they break. Source new parts carefully. Choose materials that have the lowest cost to the earth.

When creating new goods, create things that solve problems. Then share what you have made by using open-source plans and the Creative Commons.

Think backward. Start by considering any manufactured thing. Track the item back to the raw materials from which it came. Note the rubber tree in the tire, the cotton in the thread of a textile, the silica in a glass pane. Search out the processes used to abstract the raw materials used to create a product. Ask questions: "How did silica become glass?" As you follow this chain of events, contemplate the energy spent, cost in CO_2 emissions, and the pollution caused. Count the labor and time invested. Consider the longevity of the product. How long is it meant to last? Thinking like this allows us to locate ourselves in a commodified world; it makes evident the repercussions of our decisions. Seeing the whole picture enables us to act more responsibly and make choices that preserve life.

Try contemplating two different objects: one natural, such as a leaf or the carcass of a bird found roadside, and an abstracted object such as an electric hair dryer or a bottle of shampoo. Observe what these objects are able to tell you about themselves. Natural objects, when contemplated, can reveal things about the laws of nature; manufactured goods mostly tell about the decisions that people have made while building a commodified world. Notice two kinds of knowledge, natural and acculturated, and consider their value.

Avoid debt. Debt makes for immobility and congestion; flow stops. Debt limits freedom — the ability to act naturally in an arising situation — by tying us to obligations from the past. Avoiding debt helps us live freely in the moment.

Avoid gossip. People who see the bright side of a situation are the beneficiaries of a luxury. They feel that they have enough. Poor manners and complaints are signs of the feeling of lack. Gossip spreads rumors that this world is not good enough, evidenced by the flaws noticed in other people. Every effect has a cause, and every cause a reason. Concealing the flaws of another gives those who act from a feeling of lack a chance to consider something different.

Seek abundance (not wealth). Wealth is related to riches, fortune, money, capital, finance, and assets. Abundance is related to bountifulness and plenty. Wealth is unreliable: markets go up and down, economies crash, money increases and decreases in value. Wealth produces worry and the need to protect one's assets as well as maintain them. Wealth does not regenerate.

Abundance is not contingent on these things. It is an experience, a gift, a felt view of the world that includes being part of it and supported by it. Abundance is not counted: it is celebrated.

Mikey and I have witnessed inspired people seek out an abundant life. They changed the work they do in the world, freed themselves of financial ties, and transformed the way they live. Once they reached genuine abundance, they took on debt out of desire for wealth. People lose their way doing things like picking up a second property for investment and a new mortgage. Then the garden is forgotten, there's no time for making cheese and wine, and goods are bought instead of made. We've seen friends turn their own cottage industries into self-imprisonment by taking on debt that caused them to turn their focus back to earning money.

Real quality of life is freedom from worry. It means working hard and having free time, growing and making high-quality food and goods, getting plenty of sleep, and having time to play and contemplate. It includes recognizing yourself as a creative being tied to the rest of life. Balance is key.

Reclaim your skills. Some people achieve their highest goals working with and for others. But too many of us go off to work knowing that what we do for employment does not fulfill our heart's desire. For many of us, working for others is something to do while figuring out what we most love to do. Apprenticing is even better. You've figured out what you wish to do and have found someone to show you the way. When you have a full-time job working for someone else and limited free time, you can easily forget to search out what you have to offer the world. Living a decommodified life is an invitation to discover what you most love to do. Not all of us have to leave our jobs to find purposeful work. Some do. If you should become voluntarily unemployed, consider reclaiming the skills you once gave to your employment. Our jobs contain morsels of our own desire that we modified to meet the constraints of a commodified world. Seek out those morsels. They contain clues that may help you discover what you most wish to do. For my job I produced events like press conferences and product launches, and I promoted my clients'

I wear gloves to protect my hands from ocotillo's sharp barbs. We sell a tincture of ocotillo, a remedy for bellyache, in our online store.

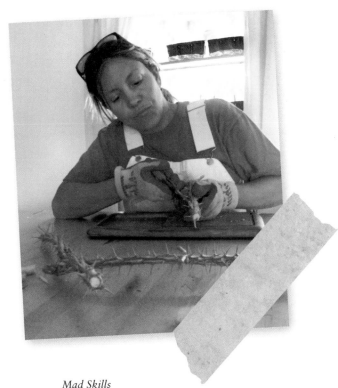

products and pitched them to the media. I turned these same skills around to create Swap-O-Rama-Rama, which required event production and promotion skills. When Swap-O-Rama-Rama became a success, free of the constraints of a profit-driven employer, I made it into a gift. After you take back your skills, you may find that you also have a gift.

Consider a cottage industry. When your time is your own and you've secured the basics (food, shelter, power, fuel, and domestic goods), you will likely have an idea about the things you would enjoy doing for the small income a maker of things needs to live abundantly.

Our cottage industry sprang up from Mikey's wish to design electronics and my desire to get to know the plant kingdom.

A successful mail-order cottage industry does require access to a post office and regular delivery by the UPS and FedEx. It also requires a good Internet connection. If you choose to live in rural areas, these simple things that are easily taken for granted can be hard to come by. Even if you are selling your goods in a brick-and-mortar environment, you can't be hauling them into town or driving 50 miles for supplies. Living in town has perks, such as a sanitation department and recycling center that offers free waste materials and dumpsters full of reusable materials. Living in a town, however small, offers amenities that make it possible to sustain a mail-order business from home.

Unbrand yourself. Our lives have formed around civilization, so naturally we take for granted the way things are. Branding and advertising are so pervasive in our culture that we hardly notice that we are being marketed to all the time.

Reclaim your home by making it an advertisement-free space. Remove or hide branding. At Swap-O-Rama-Rama events, branding on clothing is covered over with new labels that say Modified by Me. In my own home I tear branding labels off and throw them away. Repackage premade goods by moving them into unmarked containers. For example, dry foods can be purchased in bulk and stored in mason jars.

Since branding divides people into socioeconomic categories, cover or remove branding on clothing. Removing branding from your body allows people to see you for who you are rather than by how much money you have (or don't have).

Abandon trend. Trend is a cycle that necessitates throwing away perfectly good things and replacing them with newly bought goods that come at the cost of money, labor, raw materials, and energy. The decommodified lifestyle of a maker of things is a shift from devouring resources to savoring them. Instead of throwing away what you have acquired, learn to appreciate goods and keep them useful even as they wear away and break down. Then consider if they have any value as a raw material. Repurpose the parts. This is especially possible if the things that you consume are made of natural materials such as wood, metal, stone, and natural fibers.

Nothing says *conformist* like trendy goods. Avoiding trend shows others that you are conscientious and considerate, and that you think for yourself.

Lighten your paper load. Life is not to be lived shuffling paper. Limit the paper files you are willing to store and manage. I choose never to hold on to more paper files than what fits in a single, smaller-than-average file cabinet drawer. If the drawer becomes stuffed, that tells me that my life has gone off balance. I regularly sift through my paper files and thin them to what is essential.

To reduce the time you spend processing the messages of advertisers, get off mailing lists. Send junk snail mail back to its sender. Tear off the back page of catalogs, the part where your address appears near the address of the sender. Circle your address and write *Remove from list* next to it. Circle the sender's address and write *TO:* next to it so the mail delivery person knows where to send it. Put a stamp on it and drop it in the mailbox.

Receive bills digitally so that your mailbox is a place for good news. Choose a few people you love and send them handwritten letters. Soon your mailbox will be filled with replies from people who love you.

Go on a temporary media fast. For a period of time avoid computers, newspapers, magazines, e-mail, blogs, and all other media. A media fast revives the emotions and the senses. If you have ever wondered how you can tolerate the violence in movies or why you do not cry when watching bad news reported by TV reporters, it is because media desensitizes us. Feeling nothing is not a natural condition. Feeling emotion is natural. A media fast revitalizes our ability to feel these natural emotions.

Get rid of the TV. There's a reason they call what is broadcast on television *programming*. Television inserts contrived ideas about life into your consciousness. Life is much greater than what's being offered — even on a gazillion channels. Turn to nature for entertainment. Nature is alive, always arising, and always new, whereas what's on TV is comparatively predictable and repetitive. If you are concerned about missing something important, choose a few web-based media and rely on them for news of the world. Choose news sources that report good news. They do exist!

Though I chose to give up TV entirely, I know that not all of what is on television is junk. Consider balance. We need only give up the things that have control over us. When balance is regained we can return to the things we gave up, with caution.

Make a pledge. A pledge tethers you to your wishes. Once you make a pledge, you might discover that the universe's department of pledge-keeping has assigned you one of its helpful employees.

Watch out for goblins. Goblins come in many forms. My goblins matched the attributes of the career I gave up. They came in the guise of fame and money. They are inevitable. When we set out to do something purposeful, and usually right when we're nearing our goal, goblins appear to ask, "Do you really mean it?" Answer, "Yes, I do," and keep moving forward toward the goal of your pledge.

Acquire fundamental knowledge. Remember what the poet Rumi said: *You are that which you seek.* Seek knowledge. Take classes in sewing, welding, woodworking, cooking — whatever sparks your curiosity.

Pick up a pocket reference guide and peruse it for fundamental information such as the periodic table, the attributes of the elements, melting points, and types of measurements.

After Mikey fixed the swamp cooler, he came inside to hem a pair of pants.

MAD ⟩⟩ ⟩⟩ ⟩⟩

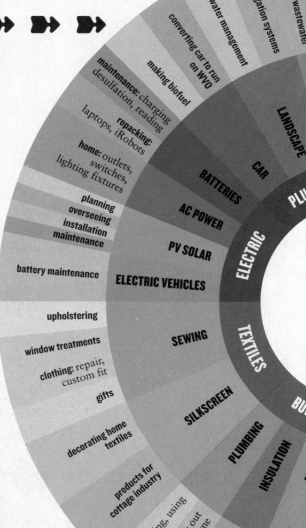

rainwater management

irrigation systems

wastewater

converting car to run on WVO

making biofuel

LANDSCAPE

CAR

PLUMB

maintenance: charging desulation, reading

repacking: laptops, iRobots

home: outlets, switches, lighting fixtures

BATTERIES

AC POWER

ELECTRIC

planning
overseeing
installation
maintenance

PV SOLAR

battery maintenance

ELECTRIC VEHICLES

upholstering

SEWING

TEXTILES

window treatments

clothing: repair, custom fit

gifts

SILKSCREEN

BUILD

decorating home textiles

PLUMBING

products for cottage industry

INSULATION

METAL

rain: catching, using

gray: water out from home

thermal mass

passive solar

chop saw

angle grinder

welder

framing saw

MIND ⟩⟩ ⟩⟩

» **SKILLS**

» » » **MAP**

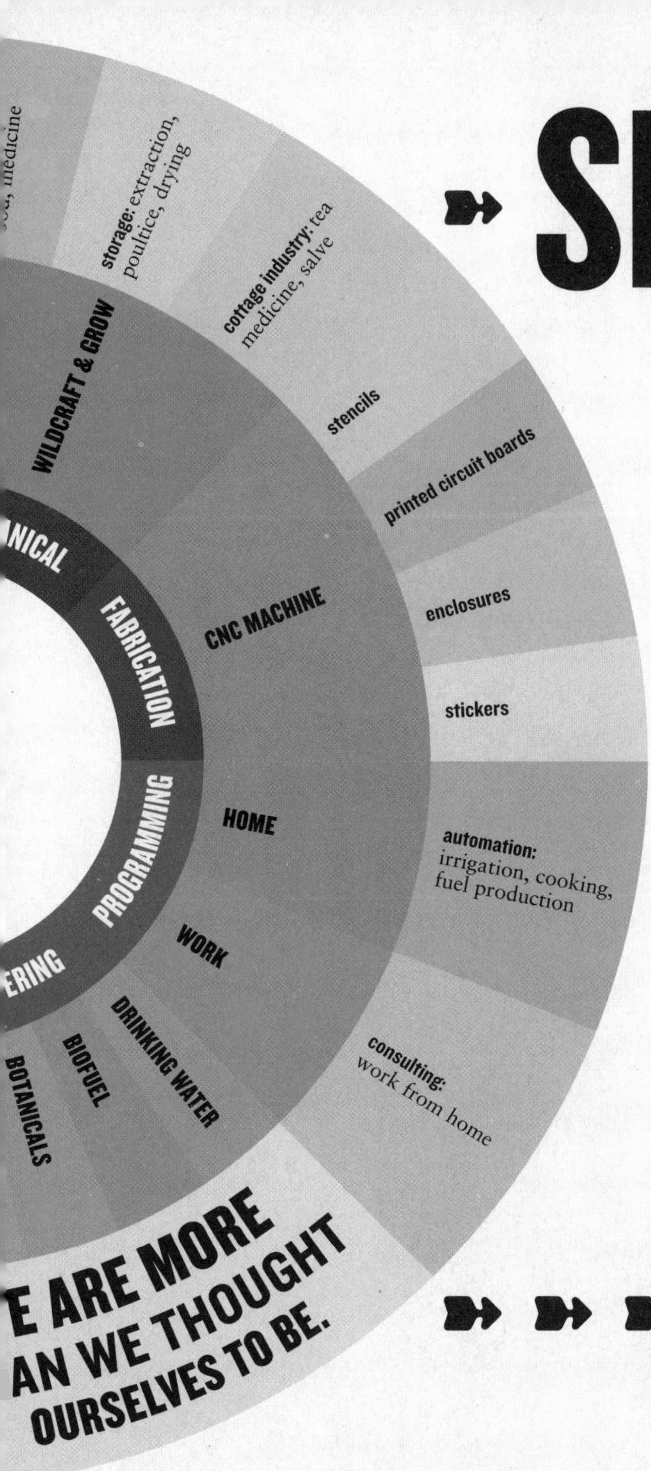

medicine

storage: extraction, poultice, drying

cottage industry: tea medicine, salve

WILDCRAFT & GROW

stencils

printed circuit boards

enclosures

...ANICAL

FABRICATION

CNC MACHINE

stickers

PROGRAMMING

HOME

automation: irrigation, cooking, fuel production

...ERING

WORK

DRINKING WATER

BIOFUEL

BOTANICALS

consulting: work from home

...E ARE MORE ...AN WE THOUGHT OURSELVES TO BE.

Know where you stand. Learn the directions (north, south, east, and west) from your home and from major landmarks. Practice the directions from different locations in your community.

Know the equinoxes and solstices. Observe the sunrise and sunset and the moon cycles. Consider your cosmic address in the solar system. Phases of the moon and the light of day and dark of night affect how much energy you have. Keep a diary of your energy levels and the phases of the moon, times of day, and seasons. This diary will reveal your place in the rhythm of nature and indicate when it is best to rest and when to apply yourself fully to a task.

Claim your own outdoor place. Find a spot in nature to visit for a few minutes every day. Earmark this spot as an extension of yourself and as your natural home. Use this space to see nature in all its forms, seasons

Elephant Butte Lake is one of the places I regularly visit to witness wildlife, the seasons, and weather.

and conditions. Be sure to show up in the rain, wind, snow, and sleet and at all times of day and night. This will help you appreciate nature, tune yourself to it, and remember your relatedness to life.

Contemplate nature. Commodified life has taken us so far from nature that we forget that we are part of it. Start each day by revitalizing your senses with 20 contemplative breaths, 5 for each of these elements.

EARTH. Close your eyes and breathe in and out through your nose. See the color of the earth: fields of wheat in autumn, yellow. Notice that the direction of this breath is horizontal. Imagine your breath extending out just above the ground and along the earth's surface. Watch it find valleys and climb mountain slopes. See it move between the small and the large, through blades of grass, and around boulders the size of skyscrapers. Let your breath spread over the whole earth and search out the magnetic field that surrounds the planet, solar energy stored in plants, telluric energy of the force of gravity, mineral in the rock, and life in soil. Notice what you have in common with it: your body has a magnetic field, gravity holds you to the earth, the plants are your sustenance and medicine, your teeth, nails, and bones contain the minerals below.

WATER. Close your eyes and breathe in through your nose and out through your mouth. See the color of water: green. Notice that, like water, the direction of this breath is downward. In nature water moves down from cloud to mountaintops to riverbeds and into oceans. It seeps into earth to reach roots and aquifers. Imagine water pouring over the top of your head, like a cracked egg that oozes over the face and body. Let it pass through you and seep into the ground below. Notice that water has delivered nutrition to you, to the life of the earth. Remember that you are made mostly of water and that your body filters water in specialized ways. Your urine contains nitrogen, a chemical element that supports the life of plants. As you consider water, think of it in all forms: mist, the water that makes up a hurricane, a tidal wave, a babbling brook. The earth is home to only one water. It circulates through natural processes; there will never be new water.

FIRE. Close your eyes and breathe in through your mouth and out through your nose. See the color of fire: red. Notice how this breath's direction is upward like a flame. Heat rises. The sun is a nuclear furnace that is millions of degrees hot. Its solar energy is stored or transmuted in the life of the earth: plants, animals, insects, and people, everything that lives. The heat of the molten core of the planet makes life possible. Light provides daytime and enables sight. Our bodies have a thermostat that keeps us in a delicate range of temperature; it burns a fever that kills bacteria. While breathing in, imagine a cauldron in your belly and increase its heat. Let the ash from the cauldron be taken by the breath as you exhale. Remember that carbon supports life by bonding to things and carrying them away. Fire transmutes heat to light.

AIR. Close your eyes and breathe in and out through your mouth. The color of air is blue. Notice this breath's direction: zigzagging like the wind. Each of us breathes a first and last breath; in between we are one of many filters that change the composition of the air of the planet. We take in oxygen that is delivered to all parts of our body. We exhale humidity and carbon dioxide. While inhaling, recognize the forms of air: wind, tornado, breeze, breath. Air carries kites and blows leaves into nooks. It enters the pores of plants and people and is felt by the cilia inside our lungs.

End your contemplation by remembering that at some level of magnification everything material is porous: bone, tissue, tree, and stone.

Nothing is impenetrable. When you open your eyes, remember your porousness and take in all you need for health and happiness. Without a clear boundary, you and what is other than you are no longer separate.

Identify local plants. Notice what grows where you live. At a party being thrown for a phycologist (algae scientist) friend of ours, we were surrounded by PhD students from an agricultural university. A guest was complaining about a fungal skin problem. While he was telling us about it, Mikey and I noticed that out the window behind him was a stand of creosote bush, one of the strongest antifungal plants in existence. I

I was surprised when I learned that the pretty shrub growing wild along the Rio Grande is the wolfberry bush, which produces goji berries, a super fruit that is quite expensive to buy.

Mad Skills

pointed to the bush. The PhD student knew the Latin name for creosote. But he did not know that the plant's alkaloids had antifungal properties that were the answer to his problem.

Pick up a local plant guide for reference. These guides point us back to nature, the truest book. Find out which plants are edible and which have medicinal value. Visit a local herb shop and ask the people who work there about the important plants of your region. Familiarize yourself with these master plants. They often contain remedies to ailments common to where you live. Replace food in your diet and remedies bought in pharmacies with natural local alternatives.

Find out where your water comes from. Water is essential to life. Know where your water comes from (a well? a town or city supply?). Learn about the aquifer, the reservoirs, the lakes, and the rivers near you. How is the water cleaned? Are there industries that use it? How many people rely on the same source you do? Is it sustainable? Find out about water conservation and recycling techniques.

Cook at home. There are few things more sensuous than food. It connects us to nature and to our senses. It costs less to buy high-quality food and cook at home than it does to buy poor-quality food that's been dressed up as fancy and prepared in restaurants. Eat only food: not chemicals, additives, or preservatives. Michael Pollan offers a simple rule for this: "Don't eat anything your great-grandmother wouldn't recognize as food."

Don't hoard. Hoarding is a response to believing there is not enough. There's always going to be more.

Hoarding unused materials keeps them out of circulation, makes them unavailable to people who need them, and weighs the hoarder down with a feeling of not being able to keep up. Take only what you need at the time and have a specific use for, and let the rest go. More will come when it is needed.

When you acquire something new, pass on or repurpose something similar that you own; this prevents clutter. I have found that the fewer things I own, the more I actually use what I own. We tend to appreciate goods more when we have fewer of them.

Give stuff away. In Truth or Consequences, dumpsters are free stores. When I lived in Brooklyn, the steps of brownstones were mini free marts stocked with items no longer useful to their previous owners. If your community does not have a way to pass on free goods, consider placing a box next to the trash and labeling it FREE STUFF to draw the attention of those who might want the goods inside.

At least once a year Mikey and I dig through the drawers and closets in our home and shed, looking for the things that have not proven useful enough to hang on to. We gather the goods not worthy of selling online and droplift them during the holiday season (see page 133).

Own (or share) tools. Things that make other things enable us to make or fix what we need.

Consider the value of labor. When choosing the tasks that are worth your time, it's important to have a way to gauge the value of the labor you are considering expending. Value is different for each of us. I keep for myself labors that I love, such as gardening and wildcrafting. I would never pay anyone to do those things for me. But some labors I love less; they not worth doing myself. A few questions can help you determine the labors to keep and those to let go of.

WHAT IS THE REAL COST OF DOING IT MYSELF? When my VW Beetle's window regulator broke and needed to be repaired, I looked up the cost of the part: $100. I added that to the cost of labor if a shop were to fix it (according to an online manual: $80 an hour at 3.5 hours): $280. Taking it to a shop included the risk that it would take a mechanic longer than the time estimated and my car might be held up for days. I decided it was worth "paying myself" to do it. I ordered the part and did the repair at home. It took me the same 3.5 hours that the repair manual projected and was not particularly difficult. Two well-produced YouTube videos made by someone who had done his own repair helped me through the process. When the other window regulator broke, a known flaw in the VW design, I fixed it in a snap without hesitation.

WHAT IF I GET IT WRONG? This can be a hard question to answer. When Mikey and I considered replacing the toilet, we thought about what would happen if we messed up. Where we live, plumbers are hard to find and it can take weeks to lure them to your home. If we messed up our install and needed someone in a hurry, we might find ourselves left in a lurch. But we also reasoned that it would not cost more to have a plumber fix our botched install if we failed than it would cost for the plumber to do the install in the first place. Since we had a second toilet, we went ahead and replaced it ourselves.

WILL I LEARN SOMETHING THAT I WANT TO KNOW? Consider whether the job offers you knowledge that you want to have. Mikey wanted to make prototypes and odd-shaped objects out of a variety of materials. He bought a computer numerical control (CNC) machine that is a digital drill press and router. It runs under the control of a computer and works by cutting away material to make objects. CNC machines can be used to make things out of wood, plastic, glass, metal, and stone. Mikey knew that it would take him at least six months to begin to learn how to use it, but he knew that he wanted to learn.

Both of us learned to weld because we knew that it opened the door to many different projects that we wanted to build ourselves, including ferro-cement buildings, furniture, art, and gates. I love plants and wanted to learn more about them, so I happily took on that study and learned to make my own medicines. On the other hand, when we lost power in part of our home, concerned about safety and the risk of fire, we hired an electrician.

DOES IT REQUIRE SPECIAL OR ONE-TIME TOOLS? When Mikey and I added up the amount of money we spent annually on wine (approximately $3,000), we knew that it was worth our spending a couple of hundred dollars on one-time purchases of specialized equipment such as carboys, bottle racks, and a corker. When Mikey was repairing a part of the grease conversion kit on our WVO Mercedes, he chopped up a tool and welded a bunch of parts to it to create a one-time-use tool because it would have been silly and expensive to buy something comparable.

DO YOU HAVE THE TIME? If you have no free time, you might not want to take on a lifestyle change that requires time. There is no point in taking on harvesting WVO, filtering it, and making it into bio-fuel if you have a full-time job and barely enough free time as it is. Making biofuel is a time-consuming practice. It might be worth buying it from a nearby maker or, if it's available, at the pump.

DOES IT CONTRIBUTE TO THE QUALITY OF MY LIFE? We value the organic tomato. We are willing to work hard for the food we grow in our garden. The garden is our health insurance plan, and it provides us with a great deal of happiness and pleasure. The labor we gave to the first year of gardening, when infrastructure needed to be built, mistakes made, and lessons learned, amounted to our being paid 50 cents an hour for our work, but we didn't mind because the garden made us happy. Each year the garden requires less labor, so the value of the time we spend on it increases.

WHAT'S THE COST TO MY BODY? We each get one body. Take care of your original equipment. Recovering from a back injury, a hernia, and other kinds of injuries can take us out of commission for a long time. If you are 25 years old, go ahead and use railroad ties for fence posts and install them yourself. But if you are older, you might want to hire someone younger to do the job. Or choose a lighter material to work with and do the job yourself.

Never lift what you can drag, never drag what you can roll, never roll what you can leave.
— JAN ADKINS, *Moving Heavy Things*

WHAT IS AVAILABLE? We have access to fresh, locally grown eggs. For this reason, we do not raise chickens. Honey is harder to come by and it is expensive, so we raise bees. Honey's high dollar value and ease to manage make raising bees worthwhile for us.

Kitchen Magic

Eating with the fullest pleasure is perhaps the profoundest enactment of our connection with the world. In this pleasure we experience and celebrate our dependence and our gratitude, for we are living from mystery, from creatures we did not make and powers we cannot comprehend.

— WENDELL BERRY

I was raised on microwaved fried chicken, chocolate milk made from powdered Quik, and Cap'n Crunch cereal. I survived the first 10 years of my life on pizza from a box that came from the freezer that my mom called the Frigidaire. No one taught me how to cook or prepare food. Looking back on the early years of my life, I remember being tired and run-down. I had frequent stomach problems, and I got sick often.

In high school I began to cook, simply because I did not want to eat what was in the freezer. In college I prepared food for groups of friends and learned the social value of feeding people. Back then I thought that by boiling pasta shells from a box, stuffing them with ricotta cheese from a plastic container, and dumping tomato sauce from a can on top, I'd cooked something that I could call homemade. Today I can hardly find a fancy restaurant that lives up to the standard to which I've grown accustomed. Thanks to my garden, local community, local farmers, and some mad skills, I eat high-quality, nutritious food all the time.

The idea that life is as interesting as your interest in it is celebrated in the kitchen. Our Holy Scrap kitchen is a lab, workshop, and teaching space. Here our garden's bounty and plants that we forage are processed and preserved, honey is separated from wax, salves and medicines are made, and live food is fermented in jars and bottles of great variety. Our kitchen is host to skill-sharing parties where our friends and community learn to bake bread, make cheeses, and process and bottle kombucha, wine, and mead. We've hosted numerous pancake- and pasta-making parties in which every hour different guests are elected to work the stove and flip the cakes, mix the batter, roll out the dough, or serve.

In the kitchen, being a maker of things offers some of the greatest rewards: financial savings, vibrant health, pleasure, creativity, and expanding knowledge of science, chemistry, biology, botany, and alchemy (to name a few). Making food and medicine produces a tangible end product that can be shared with friends. Like magic charms, making and gifting food invite friendship and abundance into your life. Give someone a loaf of bread, a bottle of homemade wine, or a cupcake, and you have gained a friend. Teach people how to make these things themselves, and you've strengthened your community.

The personality of our kitchen is a reflection of our diet and lifestyle, which shapeshifts to match what our garden has produced, what local foods are available, how our health is, and what the conditions of the world are. When Mikey and I lived in New York City, we were vegans; that helped us skirt many of the downsides of industrial food production. In New Mexico, with different options, we eat animal products. When we befriended a farmer who raises a couple of dairy cows, our objections to dairy disappeared and we began making our own raw cheese and yogurt. Experimentation with diet can reveal a food allergy and the need to modify one's diet. Whenever another fruit or vegetable is added to the list of genetically modified foods, we make a new effort to avoid it or seek an alternative.

Mikey and I are slow-food eaters, by which I mean that all our meals are made at home from scratch and from raw ingredients mostly from our region, grown in our garden, or foraged nearby. We favor local indigenous plants for food and medicine, and enjoy live and fermented foods active with microorganisms. We raise several cultures in our kitchen, including three varieties of kombucha (jun, red wine, and a common variety), kefir, yogurt starter, koji (for making sake, miso, and tamari), and we keep on hand meso- and thermophilic cultures to make cheese.

The few recipes that I share in this book are meant to point you in the right direction; you will develop your own favorites informed by where you live and who you are. You'll want to think about healthy replacements for junk food; beverages so delicious, nutritious, and interesting that you will forget about store-bought drinks completely; living foods that are also medicinal; unusual ways to process food; quirky tricks and techniques; ways to make foods that are not available in stores; things that you must make yourself in order to include them in your diet. We also provide tips about using freely obtained local plants.

A highly functional kitchen capable of processing sophisticated food and medicine starts with good tools. On the following page is a list of the more unusual tools we consider essential. (We've left out the obvious, things like the potato peeler and the paring knife.)

Tuesday seems to be our catch-up-on-cooking day. This week we made kombucha, yogurt, Chihuahua cheese (semi-hard, somewhat like cheddar), mesquite molasses, and racked wine.

Kitchen Magic

KITCHEN TOOLS

- **VACUUM SEALER.** Removes air from bags and mason jars
- **OXYGENATOR.** Produces oxygenated water used for household cleaning; removing bacteria, molds, and fungus from produce; and sterilizing bottles for storage of homemade beverages
- **STOVETOP SMOKER**
- **THRIFT SHOP POPCORN MAKER.** Roasting coffee (see page 229)
- **SEVERAL COFFEE GRINDERS.** Grinds seeds, nuts, dried plant roots, coffee
- **DIGITAL THERMOMETER.** With a probe and temperature-based programmable alarm
- **HAND-CRANKED PASTA MAKER**
- **HIGH-POWERED BLENDER.** Model with a strong motor seconds as a hammer mill
- **LARGE FOOD PROCESSOR**
- **TEMPERATURE CONTROLLERS.** Controls temperature of environments for fermenting and making yogurt, bread, wine, and cheese; convert chest freezers into refrigerators (see page 170)
- **STAINLESS STEEL WIDEMOUTHED FUNNELS.** Various sizes
- **PRESS.** Homemade jack press or an AeroPress for filtering liquid extractions
- **JUICERS.** Handheld juicer for large citrus, a small juice press for lemons and limes, and a powerful electric juicer for most other fruits and vegetables
- **STAINLESS-STEEL COMPOST BUCKET.** With lid
- **ELECTRIC DISTILLER.** For drinking water, tincture making, and refilling battery cells
- **A LOCAL PLANT BOOK.** Our favorite food book, *American Indian Food and Lore: 150 Authentic Recipes,* by Carolyn Neithammer, we found on Amazon for $1.65. If I were heading into the desert to live off the land and could bring only one thing, I would bring this book.

BEVERAGES

"The average American consumes 44.7 gallons of soft drinks annually," Mark Bittman reported in the *New York Times* in July 2011. Based on the supermarket price of $2 a gallon, the average American household (a family of four) spends about $500 on carbonated sugar (most likely high-fructose corn syrup and water.)

Considering that most households consume other beverages, too — coffee and tea, summer drinks, fruit juices — it is easy to estimate that many households spend thousands of dollars a year on beverages. This number can be reduced to next to nothing. At the same time, the quality of the beverages can be healthful and even medicinal. Homemade beverages connect us to the natural environment and are free of preservatives, additives, and packaging. Delicious, too!

We use a French press to filter beverages before storing in quart-sized, widemouthed mason jars.

Kitchen Magic

FREEZE 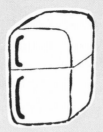 and then thaw

$1/3$ = The first third of the mass to thaw is concentrated juice.

$2/3$ = The remaining two-thirds is mostly water.

Pour the $1/3$ off into ice cube tray and REFREEZE for future use.

The $2/3$ that is mostly water can be consumed as a refreshing, mildly FRUITY drink.

Fruit Drinks

Seek out locally grown fruit. If you have land, grow your own fruit trees. If you are starting from saplings, consider dwarf fruit trees that produce fruit in just a couple of years. Many people who have fruit trees are inundated by the bounty they produce and are willing to share it, if you pick the fruit yourself. We attend an annual grape crush and show up with buckets to pick apples and cherries from friends' orchards. Pomegranates grow well where we live and are favorites for homemade juice blends. Prickly pear cactus plants grow wild in the desert of southern New Mexico. Each year we wait for the plant to produce its tuna, a small, delicious purple fruit with medicinal properties. After a day of fruit picking, we immediately process our bounty, making and freezing juice and juice concentrate. We add juices to our homemade mead and kombucha to add complexity and sweetness to their flavor.

In the following recipes, substitute ingredients local to where you live. For example, prickly pear cactus can be swapped out for a local berry or cherry; chipotle can be swapped out for a pepper variety grown in your region.

Prickly pear cactus fruits are also known as tunas. Harvest with tongs and gloves!

JUICE CONCENTRATE ICE CUBES

Frozen juice concentrate can be used all winter long to make beverages. Also, a couple of cubes tossed into a blender with ice, a bit of honey, and a sprig of mint make a great fruit drink year-round. Through a process called fractional crystallization, you can freeze juice and then thaw it partway, releasing concentrated juice.

1. Freeze fruit juice. We like to use gallon freezer bags because you can lay them flat (we always need more freezer space) and later reuse them.

2. Begin to thaw it. The first third of the mass to thaw is concentrated juice. Pour this off into ice cube trays and refreeze it for future use.

3. The remaining two-thirds is mostly water and can be consumed as a refreshing, mildly fruity drink.

CHILLED PRICKY PEAR PUNCH

A hydrating, calming summer drink. Promotes perspiration and cleanses the skin.

1. Fill blender with 2 quarts cold water and then add 3 ice cubes of frozen prickly pear juice concentrate, 1 tray of ice, 1 teaspoon chopped ginger, 8 fresh mint leaves (or 1 teaspoon dried), 4 finger-lengths lemongrass, juice of 2 limes, 3 tablespoons your favorite sweetener, and a pinch salt.

2. Blend, strain, and serve.

Teas

Tea can be made from a variety of easily grown garden plants, including hibiscus, holy basil (tulsi), mint, hyssop, anise, fennel, lemon balm, chamomile, edible lavender, strawberry and raspberry leaves, rose hips, bee balm, caraway, cinnamon, citrus peel, dandelion, echinacea, ginger root, horehound, kava, lemon grass, licorice, nettle, yarrow, sage, and verbena (to name a few).

We make a variety of medicinal teas from wildcrafted plants that grow in the Chihuahuan desert. We supplement with plants from our garden.

Our west-facing mint has reached a point where I can start harvesting reasonable amounts. Today I went easy on it, just picking enough for a single dehydrator tray.

HOT MAPLE MINT CREAM TEA

Warming on chilly days. Relieves headache and bellyache.

1. Boil a quart of water.
2. Add ¼ cup (fresh, slightly less if dried) your favorite variety of mint.
3. Let steep for 10 minutes, then strain. Add 3 tablespoons maple syrup and 2 tablespoons cream before serving.

HOT SPICY CITRUS GINGER TEA

Perfect during cold and flu season. Boosts the immune system, opens the sinuses, and relieves sore throat.

1. Boil a quart of water.
2. Mince a thumb-sized piece of ginger and add along with 1/3 teaspoon powdered chipotle, juice of 1 lime, a pinch salt, 3 tablespoons honey, and stir.
3. Let steep for 10 minutes, then strain.

PERKY TEA

Vitamin C packed. A noncaffeine stimulant. Opens bronchial passages and soothes head- and bellyaches.

1. Mix equal parts dried ephedra plant, hibiscus, and mint.
2. Let steep in boiling water for 10 minutes, then strain. Sweeten with honey to taste. Serve hot or over ice.

NOTE: *Ephedra is a strong herb and should be used with caution. Do not use if you are sensitive to stimulants, have a heart condition or high blood pressure, or are pregnant. Not suitable for children.*

GRAVITY-FREE TEA

Antioxidant tea revivifies the adrenals, clears the lungs, relieves headache, and contains vitamin C.

1. Mix equal parts by volume holy basil, hibiscus, mullein, and mint.
2. Let steep in boiling water for 10 minutes, then strain.

Coffee

At Holy Scrap we enjoy heroic doses of caffeine. We are sticklers about our coffee's taste and care about how it is roasted. Poorly roasted coffee tastes burned and contains acids that upset stomachs.

Roasted and ground coffee costs up to three times the price of green coffee beans. Home-roasted coffee is economical, can be fine-tuned to your tastes, and makes an excellent gift. A good roast takes finesse and a developed skill.

Coffee roasters are expensive, often several hundred dollars. Sticking to our ethic of living in the waste stream, Mikey and I roast green coffee beans in old popcorn makers that we find at thrift shops and garage sales. The poppers usually cost us between $1 and $3. Not all are appropriate for this task. The right popper must have two features: the cylinder (whose sides near the bottom must be perforated) and a solid (not perforated) base. The best-known and favored model for this task is the Poppery I.

Mikey was pretty happy with our eBay purchase of green coffee beans — an 8-pound bag of Guatemala Prime.

ROASTING COFFEE BEANS

Always roast coffee beans outdoors to release the CO_2 the process generates.

1. Place ²/₃ cup of green coffee beans in the popcorn maker's cylinder and run the machine until the beans are properly roasted. You will know the beans are ready when they turn dark and are oil-coated, and you hear a frequent crackling sound. It takes approximately 8 minutes to roast the first batch. (If you roast another batch, that and any subsequent batches will probably take half the time, because the metal cylinder in the popcorn maker is already warm.)

2. When the beans are done, immediately put them in a metal strainer to cool, or they will taste burned.

3. Keep the beans in the strainer (or an open container) for 48 hours so that they off-gas the CO_2 produced. Otherwise, it will be reabsorbed by the beans and make an acidic coffee that will hurt your belly.

TIP: *A pinch of cardamom added to a hot cup of coffee reduces its acidity.*

We picked up this Poppery II for $1 at a yard sale.

Milks and Smoothies

Milk does not always require a cow! Nut milks and creams are high in protein and delicious. Here are a few of our favorite nondairy milk and cream recipes.

DATE ALMOND VANILLA YOGURT SMOOTHIE

This substantial high-protein beverage can replace a meal. It tastes like autumn smells.

1. Soak ½ cup raw almonds overnight.
2. In the morning drain the water and rinse a few times.
3. Puree the nuts in a blender.
4. Add 2 cups yogurt, 1 cup cream or milk, 1 tray ice cubes, 4 pitted dates, ¼ teaspoon vanilla, a sprinkle of nutmeg and/or cinnamon, and blend until smooth.

Protein-rich cashew cream is yummy over berries, especially with cacao shavings on top.

NUT MILK

Coconut and nut milks are simple to make and lovely alternatives to animal milks. Like animal milks, nut milks contain protein. Try choosing a local nut. Where we live, pecans and pine nuts are easily obtained during harvest season, though our favorite sweet nut milks come from cashews and almonds.

1. Fill ⅓ of a lidded glass jar with raw nuts or coconut shavings. Fill the rest of the jar with water and place the lid on.
2. Soak the nuts or shavings overnight.
3. In the morning, strain and discard the water they soaked in. Rinse the nuts a few times with fresh water.
4. Mix the nuts or shavings with hot water so that the ratio is 1 part nuts or shavings to 2 parts water. Blend in a blender on high; strain; store in the refrigerator.

NOTE: *Instead of throwing away the strained coconut or nut pulp, try spicing it in a frying pan and using it to replace cheese and meat filling in raviolis.*

DESSERT CREAM

This is similar to whipped cream, but far more nutritional. Try this rich cream over berries with shavings of cacao bean and hazelnut.

1. Soak raw cashews overnight.
2. Drain and discard the water they soaked in. Rinse the nuts a few times with fresh water.
3. Whip the hydrated nuts in a blender with a bit of honey.
4. Add a bit of water if necessary to obtain desired texture.

Beverage Storage

Corkers and cappers are inexpensive tools that help preserve home-made beverages. An oxygenator is an appliance that creates oxygenated water that can be used to clean the difficult-to-access interiors of reused bottles obtained for free from local restaurants or saved from previous wine purchases. All you need is a few sprays of oxygenated water swished around inside the bottle and then poured out.

Bottled homemade drinks are impressive gifts to bring to parties and potlucks. Customize the bottles with your own labels.

Last week we bottled our second batch of homemade wine, a shiraz. For this label I hand-drew the image because I really wanted it to look like our cat.

LIVING AND FERMENTED FOODS

Mikey and I are fans of author and fermentation fetishist Sandor
Ellix Katz. He has written great books on home fermentation: *Wild
Fermentation: The Flavor, Nutrition, and Craft of Live-Culture Foods*
and *The Art of Fermentation*. In his books, Sandor advocates eating
foods that have active bacteria and contain enzymes symbiotic to our
body's flora. Sandor describes some of the benefits of living foods as
follows:

> **DIGESTION:** microorganisms break down nutrients into more
> digestible forms
> **NUTRITION:** microbial cultures create vitamins through
> conversion
> **PROTECTION:** many organisms protect us from more harmful
> organisms and substances
> **PRESERVATIVE:** they produce alcohol and lactic and acidic
> acids

Fermented and living foods are often impossible to find in stores. Laws
that require foods to be pasteurized (heated to temperatures that kill
bacteria and make enzymes inactive) make some live foods illegal.
Unpasteurized milk, for example, is illegal in most states. If you want
to eat living foods, it is best to raise your own cultures. If you are new
to fermentation, be sure to grab a good guidebook for tips on how to
work safely in the world of microorganisms.

Some people believe that harmful microorganisms exist only in food
that is manufactured and processed by large-scale systems. Most of the
food produced in America is manufactured in this way, and so pasteuri-
zation is an accepted standard and law for dairy products. Honey, fruit
juice, cheese, and yogurt are commonly pasteurized, but there is no
legal requirement to do so.

We've found it safe and enjoyable to live with microorganisms. We have obtained microorganisms —bacteria, yeast, and fungus — on the Internet, networked to get them from friends, and traded them. Cultures are part of our domestic economy. See the next spread for some of the microorganism we keep alive in our kitchen. Mesophilic organisims thrive at moderate tempratures, and thermophilic organisms thrive with heat.

THREE-DAY LACTO-FERMENTED KIMCHI

Our lacto-fermented kimchi *cooks* vegetables enzymatically. Imagine that the microorganisms work with the enzymes (a chemical catalyst) to predigest your food. While the traditional process of making kimchi takes months, our lacto-fermented kimchi is ready to eat in three days. It is full of healthy probiotics and high in vitamin C. And did I mention that it's delicious *and* inexpensive?

1 head your favorite cabbage

1 pound carrots

8 cloves chopped garlic*

2 tablespoons minced ginger

2 tablespoons sesame oil*

2 teaspoons salt

½ teaspoon dry red pepper flakes

juice of 2 limes

approximately 1 pint kefir whey (see page 243)

1. Shred cabbage and carrots and fill mason jars with the mix. Press them down with the back of a spoon to pack the jar tight.

2. Mince the garlic and ginger in a bowl with sesame oil, salt, red pepper flakes, lime juice, and kefir whey that has been inoculated with a spoonful of kefir culture. Any whey that

Airlocks on the mason jars allow natural gases to leave without letting air in.

contains a live culture will do. Live cultures can be obtained from yogurt, a live cheese, or kefir.

3. Pour the liquid mixture over the cabbage and carrots, being sure all the vegetables are covered in the liquid. Leave a little space at the top for expansion. Cap tightly and store at room temperature, away from sunlight.

4. After approximately 24 hours, the mason jar lid will pop up from pressure. When this happens the jars are ready to go into the refrigerator.

Refrigeration slows down the fermentation process.

FINISHING: After three days in the fridge, the culture has fermented the vegetables and spices in the jar, and your kimchi is ready to eat. Serve over rice.

NOTE: *The liquid in the jar will bubble and carbonate. Open the jar slowly. Like a bottle of champagne, it can flow over.*

*Garlic can be swapped for onion, and sesame oil for fish oil.

LIVING
AND

Cheese
and Yogurt
mesophilic or thermophilic
culture + milk

Wine
yeast
+
fruit

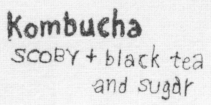

Kombucha
SCOBY + black tea
and sugar

FERMENTED FOODS

Kimchi
unpasteurized whey
+ cabbage and vegetables
+ spices

Tempeh
fungus + soybeans

Mead
yeast + honey

Kombucha

We raise microorganisms that produce a nutritional drink commonly called kombucha. A kombuch culture, called a *mother*, looks like a round, slimy, rubbery disc, though actually it is made up of millions of symbiotic microorganisms. It's also called SCOBY, which stands for symbiotic colony of bacteria and yeast. Kombucha mothers convert sugar blended with tea into a naturally carbonated drink that contains probiotics, a bunch of B vitamins, and antioxidants. The best way to acquire a mother is to find someone who makes kombucha. Since each batch produces new mothers (they're called daughters), makers of kombucha will have spares.

CAUTION: If your mother catches a mold, throw it and the kombucha batch away. If you are unsure, look at images on the web. Molds usually have a texture and color of their own, and they grow on top of the mother.

Prickly pear kombucha. Oddly enough, this tastes exactly like a watermelon Jolly Rancher.

KOMBUCHA

This recipe produces four 34-ounce bottles. If you drink one bottle a week, by the time you've consumed a batch, your next round of kombucha will be just about ready for bottling. Don't forget to share the daughters.

1. Brew 4 quarts of black tea and add 4 cups of white sugar. Over low heat, stir until the sugar is completely dissolved.

2. Remove the tea from heat and let it cool.

3. Pour the room-temperature tea into a widemouthed glass container. This is where the sweetened tea will be transformed into the sparkling fermented drink that is kombucha. Add the mother. Cover the glass container's opening with a cotton cloth held in place with a rubber band.

4. Store in a cool place out of direct sunlight. Wait 14 days and then check the taste. Always use a clean spoon and never double-dip, because your mouth's bacteria can contaminate the mother. If the tea is too sweet, wait a few more days and taste it again.

5. When the tea has achieved a taste you like, it is ready to bottle. Take the mother out of the container and place it in a clean bowl. Just before bottling, add a juice concentrate of your choosing, to taste. Our favorite is prickly pear cactus juice concentrate. Second to prickly pear, we favor local pomegranate juice.

6. Pour the kombucha tea into swingtop bottles to store it. Swingtop bottles are secure and will not pop open due to the release of CO_2 that takes place during carbonation. As you are ready to drink the tea, move the bottles to the refrigerator.

7. If you wish to make vinegar, let the kombucha mother sit longer. When the sugar is completely eaten up, vinegar remains.

8. Immediately begin the cycle again, storing the kombucha mother in a tea-and-sugar blend.

Wine and Mead

Few things are more exciting and empowering than making homemade aphrodisiacs such as wine and mead. People are wildly impressed when they receive a bottle, whether it's made from vintage grapes, dandelions, clover, or honey. While we wait for our fruit trees to grow at Holy Scrap, we've been learning about winemaking by using wine kits. Kits have taught us the process, showed us the ingredients and additives used, and helped us understand the things that affect the taste.

MEAD

Making mead is alchemy. For the cost of 3 pounds of honey and some of your time, you can produce a hundred dollars worth of wonderful mead, a sweet alcoholic beverage. Unlike most beer, mead is gluten-free and hard to find. It makes a special gift.

2 (1-gallon) glass jugs

approximately 1 gallon water

3 pounds plus ½ teaspoon honey

plastic airlock

yeast (Champagne yeast, for a relatively dry mead)

4 to 6 wine bottles and corks or 4 to 6 swingtop bottles

1. Heat ½ gallon of water to 100°F and mix well with 3 pounds of honey in a 1-gallon jug. Put an airlock on the jug's opening and let stand for 24 hours.

2. Add water up to the base of the neck of the jug.

3. Heat ½ cup of water to 100°F and mix with a ½ teaspoon honey. Sprinkle yeast on top of the water mixture to activate the yeast. Let yeast activate for 30 minutes before adding it to the honey–water mixture in the jug.

4. Return airlock to the jug's opening and let sit for 3 weeks away from sunlight in a moderate temperature room in your home (78 to 82°F is ideal).

Making kit wine requires one-time equipment purchases — things like a hydrometer (a tool that measures the amount of alcohol in liquids), a carboy (a large glass container), a plastic bucket, and a corker. All of these can be found at wine supply stores; some starter kits include them. Wine kits come with the grape juice needed to make wine. You can choose your favorite varieties: chardonnay, pinot noir, zinfandel, and others. Kits cost well under $100 and produce 30 bottles of wine. Wine bottles are easily obtained from local restaurants and can be reused over and over again.

5. After 3 weeks, the mead is fermented. Dead yeast will have settled at the bottom of the jug. Remove the airlock and carefully pour the jug's contents into a second 1-gallon jug, leaving the bottom layer of sediment behind.

6. Top off with water, this time filling the neck of the jug. Return airlock to the jug's opening and let stand for 2 more weeks.

7. Pour the mead into wine bottles, leaving behind any sediment and leaving a little room for expansion. Seal each bottle with a cork or use swingtop bottles. When bottling, you can add flavor in the form of a fruit concentrate. Add concentrate one tablespoon at a time until the taste is to your liking. The added sugar in juice concentrate helps carbonate the mead and bring out its flavor.

FINISHING AND STORAGE: Aging is critical. Let the mead sit for at least 3 months after bottling. Temperature matters; to get a good carbonation during this anaerobic stage, store your mead in a place where it can maintain 72°F. To help the cause, consider wrapping the jug or setting it on a small electric heating pad.

Dairy

At Holy Scrap we make our own dairy products. We have found that unpasteurized milk and cheese made from raw milk is easier to digest than pasteurized dairy products. Because unpasteurized milk and cheese are illegal in most of the United States, we consume them at our own risk. To obtain raw milk, we tell the farmer who sells it to us that we are buying it to feed to our pets. Some states allow people to buy a share in a cow and consume that cow's milk.

Each week we buy two gallons of fresh raw milk. We pour the cream at the top of each gallon into mason jars for coffee and sauces. The rest we transform into soft mozzarella cheese, cream cheese, butter, and a cheddar or aged hard Romano. We flavor soft cheeses with sun-dried tomatoes, roasted garlic, or chives — simply by blending it with these ingredients in a food processor pulsed a few times. The beautiful, richly textured, living cheeses we make have more flavor than any artisanal cheese we have been able to afford.

Cheese making requires either a mesophilic or thermophilic culture and rennet. The type of culture depends on the type of cheese you are making. Buy a cheese-making book to guide you. As with wine making, you'll need to make just a few one-time purchases, items that come in beginner starter kits.

Unprocessed cheese remains in a malleable state. When our home-made cream cheese or mozzarella starts to sour from sitting around too long, I fry it in oil to transform it into something similar to a fresh cheese common in South Asia called paneer.

YOGURT. When our kitchen is stocked up with homemade cheese, we use milk to make yogurt by inoculating a mason jar of fresh farm milk with a spoonful of yogurt. We place the activated mix in our homemade fermentation chamber and use the temperature controller that Mikey designed (see page 170) to hold the chamber at a temperature of 109°F. Twenty-four hours later, drain the excess fluid by straining over a cloth

I also like to make my yogurt using a water bath technique. It's quick (only about five hours), and the yogurt takes on a smooth texture that I love.

napkin in a colander. The end result is delicious yogurt full of healthful probiotics.

WHEY. Making cheese produces a by-product called whey, a protein-rich liquid full of probiotics. We use kefir whey to make kimchi (see page 234) and feed our pets, and if ever I suspect that I have a vaginal yeast infection, I fill a douche with the whey. It balances out the yeast and bacteria in my body and adds good probiotic microorganisms to the body's flora. Used in this way, it is a natural and inexpensive remedy with no negative side effects.

Protein

When wild game is available, we enjoy dishes made with animal protein. In between, our staple sources of protein are nuts, beans, mushrooms, and tempeh.

TEMPEH

Tempeh is our favorite soy-based protein. Made of soybeans bound together by a fungus, it has a delicious, nutty flavor and makes a great meat substitute in dishes such as stir-fries. We also use it in sandwiches. Asian cultures call it the "meat of the fields" because it is a high-protein delight that can replace meat in many recipes. Because making tempeh is a long process with many steps, we make large batches and freeze it in meal-sized packages. Tempeh starters can be purchased on the Internet.

32 ounces dry soybeans

large metal pot

water

cooking thermometer

food processor

colander

tempeh starter

12 zippered sandwich bags

fermentation chamber (see page 255)

1. Place the soybeans in a large metal pot. Fill the pot with water and soak overnight.
2. In the morning, pour off the water and refill with fresh water. Boil the beans on a stovetop or in a solar oven (at 300°F) for at least 1 hour, until tender.
3. Strain off the water again. Transfer the beans to a food processor and pulse three times.
4. Place the semichopped beans back into the metal pot and fill with water. Drain again, and

Mushrooms are fun to grow at home. An exotic variety of spores can be purchased on the Internet.

rinse 5 times before pouring the beans into a colander to drain a last time. This process winnows the skins off the beans.

5. Transfer the skinless beans to the metal pot and heat to 90°F. Inoculate with 2 tablespoons of tempeh starter. Stir well.

6. Use a fork to make many small holes in the sandwich bags. Cover the bags in holes as though making a wallpaper pattern. Fill each bag ¾ full with the inoculated tempeh mix and flatten out the bag so that the tempeh bricks are 1 inch thick. Place the bags in a fermentation chamber and set the temperature controller at 90°F for 24 hours.

7. After 24 hours, begin checking the tempeh. Look for a white fungus growing between the beans. The fungus will glue the beans together, forming a solid, bricklike mass. When the white fungus begins to show speckles of black, you know that your tempeh is ready. (This black tempeh fungus is not a sign of a problem.) Pull the tempeh bags from the fermentation chamber and freeze.

SERVING: If you are adding tempeh to a stir-fry, try frying it until browned and crispy with chopped garlic, tamari, and honey. Then crumble or cut it into 1-inch lengths and serve over steamed veggies. Tempeh is wonderful on a sandwich with fresh greens, a slice of tomato, and your favorite dressing or condiment.

BAKED GOODS

You would think that making pasta, bread, crêpes, and other baked goods is hard to do because so few people do it. Baked goods are easy to make, inexpensive, and delicious. It's amazing what you can do with time, flour, and an egg.

Make Your Own Flour

These days, many people are finding out that they are healthier cutting wheat flour out of their diets. Whether you're a celiac or you'd just like to eat a more varied diet, flour is a good place to experiment with alternatives. Also, stored flours often contain molds that cause health problems. You can make your own nut, coconut, bean, and rice flours by grinding them in a blender or a coffee grinder. Find out if there is a plant that grows in your area that can be used as an alternative to wheat flour. Consider mixing this local flour into recipes. In southern New Mexico, mesquite trees are commonplace, so we grind mesquite bean pods to make a nutritious flour and add it in portions of one-third mesquite flour to two-thirds white flour in any recipe. This is a good ratio to use when mixing alternatives and wheat flour.

It'll take some experimenting to come up with flours you love. Once you do, it's easier than you might think to make your own breads, pasta, and pancakes. Once you start making your own doughs, a world of possibilities opens. Dumplings, egg rolls, phyllo, and ravioli dough; fancy breads like brioche; and rolls and baked treats like muffins, cakes, and cookies are variations of the same basic theme of flour and egg. To add extra nutrition to baked goods, add the pulp left from juicing fruits and vegetables and making coconut and nut milks. Nut and coconut pulp can be spiced in a frying pan and used as a filling for vegan ravioli.

VANILLA EXTRACT

Today it is harder than ever to find vanilla extract that actually comes from the vanilla bean. Products sold as vanilla extract are often composed of sugar and artificial flavoring. But vanilla extract is simple to make at home and inexpensive. You need only a glass bottle, vanilla beans, and vodka or another flavorless high-proof alcohol. Vanilla beans can be purchased online. Enough beans to make 50 bottles of real vanilla extract can be bought for the price of a few bottles of the mimic sold in the stores.

1. Split 6 vanilla beans in half along their length and remove the seeds by scraping them out with a butter knife. The seeds can be added as flavoring to other treats, such as ice cream or cashew cream.

2. Place deseeded beans in a lidded bottle or jar. Fill with flavorless alcohol. From time to time, shake it. As the alcohol extracts the vanilla flavor from the bean, it turns brown and darkens. The longer it sits, the stronger the extract will taste.

Making your own vanilla extract requires just a few vanilla beans, alcohol, and a jar.

STORAGE. Mikey and I keep a bottle of alcohol and vanilla beans on the kitchen counter. As we use the extract in recipes, we simply add alcohol to make up for what was used. When the color of the liquid is no longer deep amber, we replace the vanilla beans.

Kitchen Magic
247

SNACKS

Store-bought snacks contain preservatives that allow them to hang around on the shelves for years. Few are made with nutrition in mind. Our homemade snacks are nutritional and hardly qualify as junk food, but they sure do satisfy the craving for it.

LIME CHIPOTLE PISTACHIO NUTS

It's hard to stop once you start eating these. We quit when the lime and spicy chipotle starts to sting our tongues.

1. Mix ½ cup shelled pistachios with juice of 1 lime, 2 pinches chipotle powder, and 4 pinches salt.

2. Swish and serve right away.

I have been experimenting with making flavored nuts using our vacuum sealer. The vacuum seems to accelerate the absorption of the liquids into the nuts.

SPICY POPCORN

Friends who have tried our spicy popcorn usually find themselves apologizing for the lack of control that follows their first bite of this savory treat.

1. Heat ¼ cup olive oil in a frying pan on a high flame.
2. Add ½ cup popcorn and cover with an upside-down metal bowl the same diameter as the frying pan. Let the kernels pop until the sound of popping slows dramatically. Flip the frying pan to transfer the contents of the pan into the bowl that served as a lid.
3. To season, add in this order: several dashes hot sauce, 2 tablespoons nutritional yeast, and 3 pinches salt. Stir with your hands. Taste, and if necessary repeat with another sprinkle of hot sauce, nutritional yeast, and salt.

LIME CHIPOTLE KALE CHIPS

Time and time again friends look at us like we're crazy when we pull out a bag of these funny-looking green chips. After the first bite they're begging for a recipe and seeds to grow kale.

1. Make a marinade: juice of 2 limes, 2 pinches chipotle, 4 pinches salt, and 1 tablespoon powdered onion.
2. Soak each kale leaf in the marinade.
3. Place on dehydrator tray. Dehydrate at 135°F for 4 hours. Season with chopped Brazil nuts for a cheesy taste.

PLANT MEDICINE

There are many good reasons to get off of a dependence on pharmaceuticals. Pharmaceuticals require trips to doctors, are expensive, and can have serious side effects. Nature is wise, free, and often simple. Plants indigenous to a region tend to contain remedies commonly needed by those who live in that geographic area. In the dry desert of southern New Mexico, many plants aid the body in maintaining hydration. Our drinking water is highly mineralized, which can cause a buildup of uric acid, and some local plants counter that, helping prevent kidney stones. In the desert, where plants are thorny, and scrapes and punctures common, many local plants have astringent and disinfectant properties. We use the pith of the ocotillo plant to make a remedy for bellyaches and gas, yerba mansa for inflammation, scouring rush for a diuretic, ephedra for a stimulant and bronchial opener, osha for toothache and fever, mullein for an expectorant, and horehound for sore throats.

To determine which local plant remedies you need, list the most common ailments in your household. Using a local medicinal plant book, match each ailment to a medicinal plant that contains the needed remedy. Look up the times of year that the plant is best harvested and the parts of the plant that contain the medicinal alkaloids. Then set out with your wildcrafting tool kit to find it.

TIPS

- Never consume a plant if you are uncertain about what it is.
- Check your plant guide to know which parts of a plant to use: leaf, bark, flower, seed, root, sap.
- Avoid plants by roadsides and ditches or near any kind of contamination or waste.
- Always collect where the plant is abundant, and never collect more than 20 percent of the amount visible to you.
- Never collect in national forests or wildlife reserves.

WILDCRAFTING TOOL KIT

small sharp knife

small shovel

small pruner/clipper

gloves

a sack or backpack to carry samples

paper bags to separate plant samples

a marker for labeling

a 20× zoom loupe for viewing the very tiny (Bausch & Lomb makes a great keychain loupe)

a guidebook

Storage

Most plants can be dried in a paper bag tacked to the wall and left alone for a week or two. I use baling wire tied to two screws at two ends of a window to make a simple line for hanging bags filled with harvested plants. The plants can also be dried out in the sun in a screened-in box. Steeping in alcohol or honey extracts a plant's medicinal properties while also preserving it for future use.

Before we built an outdoor dehydrator, I dried plants in paper bags.

Tinctures

Most plants give up their medicinal properties to a combination of water and alcohol. Some plants require more water, and others more alcohol. Local medicinal plant books give exact ratios for each tincture. Simple extractions can be achieved with the broad rule of 50 percent water and 50 percent alcohol.

Begin by filling any size mason jar with chopped fresh plant. Your medicinal plant book is a reference for the part of the plant to use: root, leaf, seed, or flower. A pint size is sufficient for a few ounces of tincture. To make a solvent, or menstruum, to extract compounds from plant tissue, mix together 50 percent high-proof grain alcohol (190 or higher) and 50 percent distilled water. Everclear, a 190 proof alcohol, can be purchased where liquor is sold and is suitable for making menstruum. Be sure the menstruum covers all the plant material in the jar and then screw on the lid. Shake the jar daily for two or three weeks, strain, and store. Test the potency of your tincture by sampling a few drops.

If you need a tincture remedy in a hurry, just follow these instructions and strain and use the tincture right away. You won't have as strong a tincture as you would if you waited a few weeks, but you will have a remedy when you need it.

Mikey and I steep horehound leaf and osha root in honey, then use the honey in hot teas as a remedy for cough and sore throats during cold and flu season.

Topical Medicines

To make topical medicines from medicinal plants, use oil instead of water and alcohol. Olive, almond, and coconut are among the most popular oils for this purpose. Let the chopped plant and oil mixture sit in a mason jar for a month or so, shaking often, and then strain and store in a dark, nontransparent container. Add a few drops of vitamin E or vegetable glycerin to preserve.

Poultices for wounds, swelling, and bruises are easily made from garden plants such as comfrey, yerba mansa, and yarrow. (Use that local plant book to determine what plants to use in a poultice.)

To make a poultice, chop the fresh plant and add it to boiling water. Steep for 15 minutes, then scoop out the plant material onto a washcloth, add a few tablespoons of the liquid, let it cool for a few minutes if it's too hot, and wrap the area of the body you wish to treat with the washcloth. Cover with a plastic bag.

One day on my way out the door I kicked a wooden chair and broke my toe. I was about to drive to the airport (I was on my way to visit a friend, who happens to be a doctor, in Los Angeles). I decided to go with the broken toe, but first I hobbled out to my garden and filled a bag with fresh comfrey. Comfrey's alkaloids mend bone. I added yerba mansa and chamomile, since they were growing nearby. I made a poultice that I wore on my foot for the 2.5-hour drive to the Albuquerque airport. When I got to LA, I continued making a poultice each morning. My doctor friend watched me curiously. By the week's end, his wife and kids were calling me a superhuman. He said, "I've never seen a broken bone heal that fast."

HERBAL SMOKE

Many plants can be smoked. If you have or are trying to quit smoking tobacco, or if you just occasionally like to smoke, consider this medicinal blend made from dried plants.

1. Mix 1 cup mullein (an expectorant), 2 tablespoons chamomile (calming), 2 tablespoons marsh mallow (adds depth), ½ teaspoon lobelia (eases nicotine withdrawal), and ½ teaspoon of hops (adds depth). For a menthol effect, add 1 tablespoon mint.

2. Makes about 20 hand-rolled cigarettes.

ROSEMARY HAIR DETANGLER

Mikey calls this recipe Rosemary's Chicken because the smell of rosemary reminds him of his mom's roasted chicken. But don't worry — there's no meat in it!

water

thumb-size piece of *Yucca elata* root (or any saponin-containing local plant)

handful of hibiscus flowers

a handful of rosemary

strainer

funnel

empty shampoo bottle

white vinegar

1. Boil ¾ of a shampoo bottle's capacity of water and remove from heat.
2. Chop the yucca root and add to the water. (If yucca doesn't grow in your area, look up local saponin-containing plants, such as soapberry or soap nut.)
3. Add hibiscus flowers and rosemary. Cover and let sit a few hours.
4. When cooled, strain the liquid and pour it through a funnel and into the shampoo bottle. Compost the plant matter.
5. Fill the remainder of the bottle with white vinegar. Use after shampooing, as a detangler that adds shine to hair. Rinse.

HOMEMADE KITCHEN APPLIANCES

Some appliances are expensive or too obscure to find, such as a fermentation chamber to let dough rise or to make tempeh and yogurt. A sous vide water bath can have a price as fancy as its name. But these devices can be made at home and require only a temperature controller and some found objects.

Fermentation Chamber

To make a fermentation chamber, place a standard lightbulb with a plug-in cord inside a camping cooler. You can drill a hole in the cooler for the light's plug or let the plug cause the lid to remain slightly open. Plug the lightbulb into the temperature controller and set the temperature as needed for what you are fermenting. Yogurt, tempeh, and dough each have different temperature requirements. The temperature controller will hold the internal temperature in the chamber.

Sous Vide

In sous vide cooking, food is cooked in vacuum-sealed plastic bags in a temperature-controlled water bath for a long time at low temperatures. Sous vide cooking breaks down collagen and protein, making for softer textures in foods that might otherwise be tough, such as parsnips, carrots, and gamey meats like deer and elk. Sous vide cooking perfectly poaches eggs and seeps marinades into meats and veggies.

A sous vide water bath can also be used to separate honey from wax. To do so, place a screen over a small bowl and pour unseparated honey and wax on top of the screen. Place the bowl, with the screen holding the honey-and-wax mixture, into the sous vide water bath and set the temperature to 118°F (to keep the honey raw and unpasteurized). Let stand. Bottle the honey that drips through the screen. The wax will remain on top.

To make your own sous vide, simply plug an inexpensive slow cooker into a temperature controller and set it to the desired temperature. Most vegetables are cooked in a sous vide for 1 hour at 185°F. Meats cook for 10 hours at 135°F.

TIP: To blacken and crisp meats cooked in the sous vide, sear the cooked meat with a small blowtorch.

Solar Oven

If you live in a sunny place and work from home, you are a perfect candidate for a solar oven. To run a solar oven at exact temperatures, you need to reposition it as the sun moves, so this requires you to be home to watch it. Good commercial units can be obtained for $200. They are also easily made out of scrap. Solar ovens reach temperatures of 400°F and can maintain specific temperatures. This is achieved by turn-

ing the unit so that it is either more or less directly aimed at the sun. A built-in thermometer shows the internal temperature. Solar ovens can be used to bake breads, cook soups, boil beans, and reheat leftovers.

LARGE OUTDOOR PLANT DEHYDRATOR

Dry climates like New Mexico's dehydrate plants quickly. How quickly your plants dry — a day? a week? — will depend on your climate. Our dehydrator is placed in the shade.

4 yards of screen

baling wire

a few plastic bread trays

1. Cut screen to make a box a few inches larger than your bread trays. Leave one side of the box open. The open side is for slipping the screen cover over the stack of bread trays. It will keep out critters.

2. Sew screen with baling wire.

3. Cut a piece of screen the size of the bottom of each tray and place on each tray to prevent drying plants from slipping through the tray's spacious pattern.

When our local supermarket went out of business, I picked up some bread trays and converted them into a dehydrator.

Power, Electronics, and Technology

We have arranged things so that almost no one understands
science and technology. This is a prescription for disaster.
We might get away with it for a while, but sooner or later this
combustible mixture of ignorance and power is going to blow up
in our faces.
— CARL SAGAN

If you are considering taking on a new technology or creating a new
device, begin by asking:
> **CAN I AFFORD IT?**
> **CAN I MAINTAIN IT?**
> **DOES IT FIT MY LIFESTYLE?**

Kill A Watt

A Kill A Watt device shows you the amount of power home appliances
use. Learning the power draw of home devices has helped us reduce our
power consumption by more than five times.

It's also important to know exactly what kind of power your home
appliances are running on. Find out where your local electric company
gets its power. Our power comes from our onsite solar array. Our
town's power — the power we'd be getting if we were still on the grid
— is a combination of hydroelectric and coal. Even though T or C is

located a few miles south of a dam that produces hydroelectric power, the hydroelectric power T or C uses is from Utah. Strange.

CNC Kits

Mikey purchased a computer numerical control (CNC) machine in kit form so that he could home-manufacture parts he had once bought for the gadgets he designs and sells in our cottage industry store. A laser cutter was an option that offered even more sophistication and a greater variety of uses . . . at the cost of $7,500. The CNC kit for $700 (including accessories and shipping) matched our budget. While the CNC machine is slower and less accurate, it is able to satisfy the needs of our home-based manufacturing. Since Mikey had the time to build and then master the CNC, buying it in kit form and assembling it himself made sense and matched our lifestyle.

Our CNC from Zen Tool Works was super easy to assemble. When something this inexpensive is available and only takes a few days to put together, it didn't make sense for us to try to build our own.

Make a New Device

There is no reason to design custom hardware when commercial products can be obtained for reasonable prices. But sometimes there is a gap in the functionality of what is available. This is a prompt to consider designing a new version. Mikey and I wanted a temperature controller that could do things that commercially available products were unable to do. Since there wasn't an open-source hardware controller able to meet all of our needs, we designed our own (see page 170). Today we run four custom temperature controllers in our house and have sold hundreds of others to people like us who needed the functionality that we built into it.

Electronics Repair

No longer are electronics the domain of engineers. The open-source movement has welcomed everyone into the world of electronics. You can understand, hack, build, and repair your own electronics. At first we have to get past things like planned obsolescence and bad designs. Planned obsolescence — the intention that a product has a limited usefulness or becomes obsolete after an unnecessarily brief time — encourages consumers to buy more goods and create more waste. Many products are designed without the user's tinkering in mind: cases are impossible to open, making items hard to fix.

Where possible, we prefer open hardware design products. These are accessible to the consumer; they are built with tinkering in mind. These products have firmware, circuit board designs, and a bill of materials that are open and available to the user.

Kits are a great example of open-source hardware. Because the user builds the product and assembles each part, he or she is more likely to be able to repair the item if it breaks. The assembly of an open-source hardware kit is a lesson in and of itself. Building a product using such a kit helps one learn about electronic components, design, and functionality. And kits cost significantly less than finished goods.

Modern homes are filled with electronics. When they break, we have an opportunity to acquire mad skills. These broken goods offer you a chance to hack and learn.

Common Problems with Electronics

Before hacking into an electronic item, disconnect the power source. Then look for the most common problems. Loose wires can be found by lightly tugging each plug and wire. They are easily repaired with a quick soldering weld. Check the vitality of your power source and/or batteries with a multimeter. Look for blown fuses indicated by a broken metal strand inside the glass tube of a fuse. These are easily replaced. Blown

Many electronic repair projects have to do with common household devices. But there are other reasons to tinker. Here, Mikey works on a flaming doorbell.

capacitors appear as cylinders that have become bulbous and expanded from pressure. Look for burn marks anywhere. If none of these common failures have occurred, then go to the online forums and look for people talking about the same issues you are having with your device.

Here are a few questions to ask before taking apart busted electronics.

IS IT UNDER WARRANTY? If it is, send it to the manufacturer for repair or replacement. Fulfilling warranties on broken goods is equal to money not spent. For each warranty upheld, fewer goods are purchased. For example, we have five digital door locks. They cost $100 each. They came with a lifetime warranty. Three of the five were replaced free under warranty — $300 we did not have to spend. Holding companies responsible for what they manufacture helps set a high standard for the quality of goods consumers expect.

CAN I REPAIR IT MYSELF? Some devices are too difficult to repair, and opening them voids a warranty or destroys them. Sometimes a device can be fixed, but to do so creates a situation in which it is impossible to put the item back together; when the repair is finished, the lid no longer fits or wires are left hanging out, and the item is rendered useless. Open your device, if it can be opened, and see if it has room for tinkering and repacking.

DOES THE ITEM HAVE RESALE VALUE? Before hacking a broken device, see if it can be sold in broken condition on eBay. When our cat knocked Mikey's iPhone into a water bowl, Mikey scratched the phone getting it open and then found that he couldn't repair it, but he was able to sell it for parts to someone who likes to tinker. He sold it on eBay in nonworking condition.

A neighbor came over with a poorly running laptop. Mikey ordered a replacement hard drive for $50, saving a $500 laptop from becoming landfill and preventing our neighbor from having to buy a new one.

IS THERE A THIRD-PARTY PRODUCT THAT CAN GET THE ITEM WORKING AGAIN?
Forums are good sources for information about third-party products. When Mikey's Apple display stopped working, he checked the forums and learned that people were having success using a new-model power supply, not the one that was designed for his display. A $200 third-party item saved his $1,200 display from becoming waste. Our robotic cordless vacuum battery packs die regularly. Mikey replaces the cells in the pack with a third-party cell instead of buying an expensive new battery pack.

Batteries

Civilization runs on power. According to Wikipedia, only 16 percent of that power comes from renewable sources. Disposable batteries are so awful for the environment that Jon Chase wrote in a *Popular Science* article titled "The Grouse: Assault on Batteries" that "disposable batteries, no matter how efficient, should be considered a controlled substance and, as such, should be sold under the same restrictions as, say, prescription drugs or guns." If we're going to use batteries, it's proper etiquette to know how to maintain them in order to prevent them from going to the landfill.

ACQUIRE. Free batteries are abundant. Many can be found in auto parts stores, at golf courses, and marinas. Auto parts stores collect dead batteries that are picked up by scrappers and recyclers. Since the fee the store gets per battery is fixed, storeowners tend not to mind if people bring in dead batteries to trade for weak ones that can be revived.

Check would-be trash batteries for those that have a reading of 12 volts or higher, and swap them for your dead batteries.

MEASURE. To revive batteries or to get the most out of the batteries that cannot be recharged, you need to know how to use a multimeter. Whether you have AAs or car batteries, a multimeter will tell you which ones are still useful. AA batteries that are fully charged measure 1.5 volts. At 1.2 volts, they need to be recharged. A fully charged car battery should read 12.3 volts or higher. At a lower reading, it needs to be charged. A 12-volt battery reading near 0 volts can be desulfated. We choose batteries with a near 12-volt reading because they turn up in the waste stream.

Mikey regularly manages our batteries. He makes sure they're kept full of water and free of crystallization.

To use a multimeter, place one of its two probes at each terminal of a battery (red is positive and black negative) and read the numbers on the device's screen. If you mix up the probes, the display will give a negative number instead of a positive one.

Large lead-acid batteries like those used in cars and PV solar systems require water and should be checked and refilled twice a year. Rainwater, like distilled water, has a low parts per million of nonwater molecules and can be used to refill batteries. A total dissolved solids (TDS) meter can be obtained for about $20 to measure the parts per million nonwater molecules in water. Water is considered mineral water if it has over 500 parts per million of nonwater molecules. Drinking water should have less than 200 parts per million of nonwater molecules. Distilled water contains less than 15 parts per million. Rainwater usually compares to water that is distilled.

When refilling batteries, wear gloves and protective eyewear. Pop open each cell cap of the battery to see if the plates are exposed or covered in a visible layer of water. If they are exposed, add water until the plate is lightly covered.

Laptops and cell phones often have lithium batteries, which are particularly sensitive to heat. (Temperatures of 40 to 70°F are ideal for batteries.) Keep these devices out of the sun.

Biodiesel is a solvent that can be used to clean the terminals of lead-acid batteries.

REVIVE. Most batteries become junk because they sit too long. Without use, crystals form on the lead plates of a battery and reduce its capacity. There are ways to revive them.

A battery desulfator is a device that generates a sonic pulse capable of breaking up the crystals that reduce a battery's capacity. Mikey designed a desulfator he calls the Power in My Pocket (PIMP), a pocket-sized device that we sell in our online store. It requires simply plugging the device into the battery (a lead for each terminal) and giving it time.

Mikey's battery desulfator revives batteries and extends their life, reducing what goes to landfill.

REPACK. Some batteries can be repacked. Weak cells can be taken out and replaced with strong cells. The devices worth repacking have battery packs that are not too crammed; a crammed device is a difficult refit. Some home appliances and power tools have spacious battery packs worth hacking. Replacement cells can be purchased online, and model numbers can be matched with the cells taken out.

Photovoltaic (PV) Solar

One night, watching the film *The End of Suburbia* brought home to us the fragility of our country's power grid. The film made us aware of the variety of forces that affect power, including an Enron power trade that once caused parts of California to experience life-or-death rolling blackouts.

Just before leaving New York City in 2003, we experienced a three-day blackout. During the outage, no one had access to money. We had what was in our pockets. The first day of the blackout was fun. Restaurants gave out free food, knowing their refrigerators were down and the food inside them would go bad anyway. In a moment of poor judgment, Mikey spent his last $26 on a pitcher of lychee sangria for a handful of friends gathered by candlelight at a bar.

By day three, people who lived high up on the 20th and 30th floors of tall buildings were struggling and tired. In the dark they counted the floors as they climbed, in order to know when they reached theirs. People used the remaining charge on cell phones to light their way down dark hallways and to find their apartment doors. Without lift pumps, water stopped flowing to those who lived above the 4th floor, and everyone started to wonder when fresh food would come. Power was returned on the third day, but not before people became aware that we were close to seeing a whole new side of life.

These experiences encouraged us to invest in a PV solar system. Since we were the first in our geographic area to have one, getting it up and running was difficult. When we approached local electricians to do the installation, they'd say, "Never did that before." Finally one said, "I can read a schematic. Sure, let's do it." And we did.

We recommend building a mini system first (see pages 270). That way you'll understand all the issues involved.

Approval by a state electrical inspector matters if you want to receive state refunds on your PV solar installation. We stood to recoup 20 percent of the cost of our system by gaining this approval. The criteria for passing inspection are difficult, especially if you have limited resources. We regularly used parts from a local auto parts store to complete the work because the parts needed were not available. The parts were similar enough to electrical parts, and they worked.

By participating in our installation, we gained valuable experience that we put to good use. Mikey has since installed several solar setups for friends and neighbors, and he regularly advises people who are considering going off-grid.

Mikey was so excited when we got our PV solar panels working to their full potential. He shut off our grid power, turned on our solar power, and ran inside to fire up an air conditioner and swamp cooler.

Once a PV system is set up, it is usually smooth sailing. PV systems are virtually self-running. It is not a pain to live off the grid. What we like about being off-grid:

- clean, onsite source of power
- no power outages
- independence
- knowledge about power as part of our lifestyle
- the ability to add electric gadgets to our lives, such as electric vehicles

---

PV Solar Tips

If you wish to get tax deductions offered by state and federal government programs, buy PV solar equipment new. Used equipment disqualifies you from these programs. Do the math, though. Depending on the programs being offered and size of your system, it still might be worth buying used equipment.

Some municipalities offer grid ties. Grid ties let you plug into the existing electric grid and sell the excess power you produce back to it. Another option is to store your power in batteries on your own property. There are downsides to grid ties. The per kilowatt price that power companies charge customers for their power use is higher than the price they pay you when they buy the excess power you produce and sell back to them. If your PV solar system is grid-tied, you'll be charged for any power you use in excess of what you produce. While producing your own power, you can get a surprisingly high electric bill. Another downside is that if the grid goes down, you will lose power even though you are producing power. Storing the power your PV system generates on site allows you to be independent. We chose to store our power in batteries rather than tie into the grid, and we have not regretted this decision.

Do not buy a system until you have an installation plan and an electrician. Find a licensed electrician you can work with. An installation

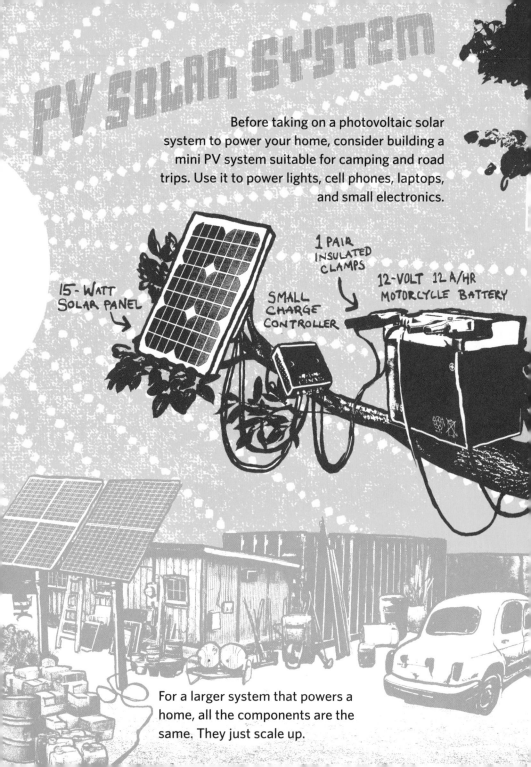

PV SOLAR SYSTEM

Before taking on a photovoltaic solar system to power your home, consider building a mini PV system suitable for camping and road trips. Use it to power lights, cell phones, laptops, and small electronics.

15-WATT SOLAR PANEL

1 PAIR INSULATED CLAMPS

SMALL CHARGE CONTROLLER

12-VOLT 12 A/HR MOTORCYCLE BATTERY

For a larger system that powers a home, all the components are the same. They just scale up.

100-WATT
POWER
INVERTER

by an unlicensed electrician will disqualify you from state and federal refunds. It is often necessary to have both an installer and an electrician. Know what you can do and what an electrician should do. You can mount the panels, dig the holes for the posts, install a pole mount (if you're using one), and hook up the batteries.

If doing a pole mount, consider how the panels will be reached and cleaned. Consider the wind patterns where you live, and avoid placement that allows the wind to get under the panels. If you pole-mount your system, consider how deep you will need to dig a hole for it.

Buy batteries after all the equipment is installed and when the system is ready to be plugged in. When batteries sit uncharged over time, crystals form on the lead plates and reduce the batteries' capacity. Know the dates that the batteries you are buying were made. Don't buy batteries made more than half a year before your purchase date. Nonsealed lead-acid batteries are considered hazardous materials and are very expensive to ship. Pick them up yourself from the supplier to save money on shipping.

If 220 power is not critical to your lifestyle, don't bother accommodating it. Adapting a PV system for 220 is expensive.

Don't run big appliances at night or when you are not producing a lot of power, such as during gray days.

Use power when you have it, because you can't save it. There are times of year in which you will produce extra power and find yourself seeking ways to use it. At other times of year you will seek to conserve power so as not to run out. You cannot store solar power beyond your batteries' capacity (the charge controller disconnects to avoid overcharging the batteries). Days with cool temperatures and direct sun produce the most energy.

When you have extra energy, use electric power where you might otherwise use gas. An electric kettle can be used to boil water. We run two electric vehicles: a golf cart for hauling heavy things around a large property and an electric car that we use for short trips around town.

When we have extra power, we run appliances such as an electric water distiller and a food dehydrator.

Before buying a PV system, spend a year studying the way that you use power. Read electric bills and find out about the sources of the power you are using. Use a Kill A Watt device to give a reading of the power consumed by the appliance plugged into it. Consider reducing the draw of the appliances that consume the most energy.

cars and fuel

Compared to vehicles with combustion engines, electric vehicles (EVs)
need very little maintenance. They need their batteries kept full of
water and frequently charged. Batteries can be maintained with just
a multimeter; they can be kept running for a long time with a battery
desulfator like the one Mikey made and we sell in our online store.
Some EV motors are rated for 1 million miles. Tires are the only parts
that need regular replacement. Since we do not favor the skill set
required to keep combustion engines running and we are comfortable
with batteries, EVs are ideal for us. We also live in a small town whose
size is a match for the distance an EV can travel before needing to be
recharged.

But we also have cars that use biodiesel that we make ourselves.
In addition to making our own fuel, Mikey and I regularly repair our
vehicles. We change bulbs in the headlights, replace window regula-
tors, maintain batteries, and change the oil and fuel filters. We've also
replaced our hood latch and recalibrated our electronic keys, to name a
couple more repairs.

Most modern vehicles have computers that you can talk to by plugging an On Board Diagnostics (OBD) device into the vehicle's port. The
right OBD device for your specific car can be ordered online. The device
will provide error codes and details as to what is in need of repair.
Decisions to repair the vehicle yourself hinge on the answers to the following questions:

- Is there a tutorial online, a demonstration of someone doing the same repair?
- Does the repair require specialized tools?
- Are the tools worth acquiring?
- Does the repair require a lift?
- What's the cost to have a mechanic fix it if you try to repair it yourself and mess it up?
- Will an error cause the vehicle to require towing?
- Do you have the time do the repair?

Weigh these answers against the cost of having the car repaired by a mechanic.

When a headlight bulb on our VW Beetle died, we picked up a replacement bulb for $5 from a local auto parts store and had the headlight working in less than 40 minutes. The dealer price is over $70.

Cars and Fuel

Fuel

Few things are more satisfying than independence from petroleum fuel and the stream of events around its production and distribution. The amount you can save by making your own fuel is tremendous — thousands of dollars a year. No more visits to gas stations!

When we first converted an old Mercedes to run on waste vegetable oil (WVO), we had many adventures. In Marfa, Texas, before heading home to Truth or Consequences, we pulled up behind a gas station that was also a diner, hoping to refuel our car from the grease pit in back. I assumed that the oil was a free waste material. So I placed one end of our grease pump into the diner's grease pit and the other end of the hose in my car's WVO tank and turned on my self-filtering pump. Since the pump filters the grease while it pumps, we pumped it directly into our converted car's WVO tank.

I casually filled our Mercedes with WVO from a grease pit behind a gas station while inside the store owner called the cops. We got out of there just in time to avoid being arrested.

Moments later a woman working at the station came out, yelling and waving her arms, a phone pressed to her ear. She paused to shout, "I called the police," pointed to the phone with her finger, and then returned to the call to review the accuracy of the directions she'd given the police dispatcher. Like Bonnie and Clyde, we bolted from the scene. As we turned off the main road and onto a side street, in my rearview mirror I saw a police car, sirens on, speeding to the scene of the crime.

Never again did I look at WVO as garbage. It is a valuable commodity. Today many biofuel makers pay restaurants for their WVO. Our Bonnie and Clyde episode happened well before the spike in the price of fuel and the stock market crash of 2008; I'm pretty sure that the woman at the station had no idea what we were doing in the grease pit. Today many of the grease pits found behind restaurants are tagged with logos and phone numbers placed on them by the greaser who has dibs on the bounty.

Etiquette is involved in being a collector of WVO. Relationships with restaurants require consideration in both directions. A greaser should promise to be reliable and tidy when picking up WVO. Set a standard and stick to it. The restaurant may promise to have its WVO prepared a certain way for you. When you are on the road, if you choose to refuel from a grease pit, ask permission before pumping. The stuff is messy. It's proper etiquette to leave no trace behind.

Some restaurants pay money to a monthly service that picks up their WVO. If you replace that service by taking it instead, you will have saved them money. Of course, once a restaurant cancels its pickup service and begins to rely on you, you have to pick up each week or make arrangements if you can't. Never leave a restaurant owner overflowing with waste oil. If you decide that you no longer need a restaurant's oil, give that account to another greaser.

When setting up a relationship with a restaurant, try to get the owner to promise to change the fryer oil every week to avoid dirty oil that has no energy left in it. Ask the owner to put cooled oil back into the same 5-gallon tote that it came in when their distributor delivered it to them. This simplifies your pickup process. If they put their oil into a big nasty grease pit in the back of the restaurant, it will be dirty, require more filtering, and be messy to pick up. A ready-to-go tote is tidy and easy. Waste oil has a long shelf life and can be stored for years.

Waste Vegetable Oil and Biodiesel

Waste vegetable oil (WVO) is oil from a restaurant fryer. Filtered WVO has been run through enough filtering that it is appropriate for making biodiesel or running in a car with a conversion kit. Biodiesel is the combination of filtered WVO and a mixture of methanol and lye, minus the glycerin by-product made by the combination. Biodiesel can be run in an ordinary diesel car without any conversion.

Once you are storing WVO at home, you can use it as sealer for outside wood, such as trim on your home, garden beds, and decks. Biodiesel can be used as a solvent and can be burned as fuel in the popular Hawaiian art called poi.

You can run a car on biodiesel during the part of the year when temperatures are over 50°F. At temperatures below that, biodiesel must be diluted with diesel fuel. As temperatures near freezing, all biodiesel should be replaced with diesel fuel.

TOOLS AND SUPPLIES. Designate an outfit for working with waste vegetable oil; it is messy work, and the stains produced by oil are lasting. Always wear protective eyewear and gloves. Never work with biofuel barefoot or with exposed skin. What you'll need:
- digital thermometer
- bucket heater (a wand that heats up when plugged into an electric outlet)
- filters (old denim jeans)

- pump (Golden Fuel Systems makes a One Shot pump that comes in a sturdy Pelican suitcase that has on-board 2-micron filtering. We recommend it.)
- funnels
- a fuel siphon
- goggles
- gloves
- 50-gallon metal drums for storage
- 5-gallon plastic totes for carrying fuel

FILTERING WITH WASTE DENIM. Denim is an excellent filter for cleaning waste vegetable oil. Most thrift shops have tons of throwaway denim, jeans too dirty or old to sell. They usually can be obtained free for the asking. There are many techniques for using waste denim to filter WVO. We straddle a pair of jeans — one leg on each side — over a stick of rebar placed across the top of a 50-gallon drum. We tie the pant legs at the ankle, fill with WVO, and simply wait for it to filter through by gravity. Each pair of jeans filters 100 gallons of fuel before finally being thrown away.

Old jeans make an excellent filter.

MAKE YOUR OWN BIODIESEL

Start with microbatches. Don't make an at-home biodiesel factory right away. For the average person, a single restaurant that gives up 5 gallons of WVO a week is all you'll need. So far, we've found that it takes us about an hour of labor (collecting, filtering, mixing) to give us 10 gallons of biodiesel, at a cost of about $1 per gallon. Here are the basic ratios:

4 gallons filtered WVO

½ gallon methanol (methanol can be purchased at auto racing supply stores)

60 grams lye

1. Before mixing biodiesel, let WVO heat up by setting the totes in the sun for a few days. During summer months, it will reach the desired temp of 132°F with solar energy. If you cannot reach temperature, it is not the right time of year to run biodiesel. Wait for warmer weather.

2. Mix methanol and lye in an open, unsealed container. Always add lye to methanol, and not the reverse. Methanol added to lye can cause an explosion. A 1-gallon plastic jug will do. By mixing the two ingredients you create methoxide. Do not cap the container. The chemical reaction caused by combining the two ingredients causes expansion that would burst a sealed container.

3. Swish the methanol–lye mixture (do not stir) until it is well blended. Pour the blend into 4 gallons of warm filtered WVO (we use a 5-gallon plastic tote). Place the tote's lid on tightly. Shake it vigorously. Then remove the tote's cap and replace it. This releases any pressure that may have built up. Set the tote out in the sun, with the cap on, for four days.

4. When you return four days later, the mixture will have settled into two layers: a light colored fuel on top and a darker

band of glycerin that sits at the bottom. Without shaking, and being careful not to remix the two layers, pour off the top layer into a storage container or directly into the gas tank of a diesel vehicle. While pouring, and as soon as you see that you've reached the glycerin layer and it is about to pour out, stop!

5. Dispose of the glycerin. Some people have made faux wood fire logs out of the glycerin byproduct. Its uses are limited, as after being mixed with methoxide, it becomes toxic. To dispose of it, reseal the container and place in the trash.

SAFETY PRECAUTION: When working with methanol and lye, always wear gloves, a mask over your mouth, and protective eyewear. Cover all exposed skin. Should you get lye on your skin, wash it off immediately with vinegar rather than water. Vinegar neutralizes the pH. Always mix methanol and lye outdoors: the fumes are dangerous.

Our very first liter of biodiesel.

Tips for Greasers

- Start with a car that's not going to fail in every possible way because it's old and terrible. Our car Chance broke down far away from home, often. Not because the WVO system we installed in it failed, but because the car was old and falling apart. We would have been better off spending more money on a newer and better working car.
- Making homemade biodiesel consumes time and requires effort. Burn homemade fuel in a car that gets good mileage.
- While any diesel car can be converted to run on WVO, it is less expensive and less labor-intensive to make homemade biofuel for an unconverted diesel car than it is to convert a car to run on straight WVO.
- Hybrid vehicles use their batteries only in stop-and-go traffic and offer little benefit to people whose lifestyle is one of driving long distances on highways. For a lifestyle of mainly long distances, a biofuel or WVO vehicle is the better choice.
- But don't expect to harvest unfiltered WVO on the road, turn it to fuel, and be off and running. To do so requires carrying filters, hauling gear, and making a mess. It's hard to come by high-quality sources of oil. Overall it is impractical and a real pain. It's reasonable to carry a tote or two of WVO or homemade biodiesel *if* you have a large enough vehicle and the storage space to hold it. And there *are* people who filter and offer WVO to others, but be sure to call ahead and find out about the provider's process. Make sure their methods live up to your standards.
- Websites like Fillup4Free.com create a network of the community of fuel makers and users. If you make fuel, filter WVO, and produce beyond your need, you can sell the extra online. If you travel in a diesel car, these sites will help you find fuel while on the road.

shelter

Do not be tricked into believing that modern decor must be
slick or psychedelic or "natural" or "modern art" or "plants"
or anything else that current taste-makers claim. It is most
beautiful when it comes straight from your life — the things you
care for, the things that tell your story.
— CHRISTOPHER ALEXANDER, *A Pattern Language*

When Mikey and I decided to build new structures, we had to decide
what material to use. Some natural builders use straw bales, and others adobe mud bricks. The soil needed to make adobe brick came from
as far as Arizona, and straw bales had to be hauled in from Colorado.
Instead, we thought about what was nearby and found a free waste
material less than a mile from our door. At the time, T or C's recycling
center collected but did not recycle the town's paper waste. Although
papercrete requires the addition of cement to make it a useable building material, and cement has a negative impact on the earth, both straw
bales and adobe mud have a carbon footprint, too, in the fuel it takes
to transport them to southern New Mexico. Both of those methods also
require a lot of labor. We would have had to hire a team to build with
us. So, with paper around the corner and an ideal dry climate, we chose
papercrete.

When setting out to build a new structure, consider what a material's impact on the earth has to do with where on earth you are standing.
Consider your climate. Begin by looking at the materials that are
nearby. Talk to local recycling and sanitation centers to find out which
materials are not being recycled, and consider how they could be transformed into building materials. Look to the natural resources of your

area, those that don't have to be trucked in. Be sure they're not scarce before harvesting them.

Find a Like-Minded Structural Engineer

Once a structural engineer signs off on a design, local building inspectors are relieved of liability and you are able to build your structure, no matter how unusual. You can build up to a certain size without a permit. But for larger structures, especially those made using nontraditional designs and techniques, it is likely that a building inspector will ask for an engineer's stamp of approval.

Before we could legally build, we had to jump through a few hoops to get our papercrete building plan approved. Initially our local building inspector asked if we were going to have our papercrete mix tested by the Underwriters Laboratory (UL). Unable to afford the thousands of dollars the UL charges to test a material's flammability, we shot a 5-minute video of Mikey holding a blowtorch to a papercrete block that I held in place. The inspector watched the video, saw that the papercrete block did not ignite, and gave us a permit to build a papercrete fence.

Building with Papercrete

Papercrete is a fibrous building material made of repulped paper, cement, and water. We were attracted to it because it makes use of a free and abundant waste material, is lightweight, and requires minimal labor. At the same time, it is super strong and insulates so well that a building made out of it costs very little to heat and cool. We knew we could do it ourselves, and it seemed an ideal material for our dry climate.

We like the variety of methods of working with papercrete: it can be poured into molds to make bricks and slabs, pumped into walls or slip forms; sprayed, troweled, and used as mortar or stucco. It works well

Though our domes are made of paper, they fit nicely into our natural landscape. Once covered in an umber-colored mortar, they look as though they're made of earth. People assume they are adobe.

with ferro-cement techniques in which armatures made of rebar and metal lath provide the frame.

The general idea is to combine equal parts (by weight) cement and paper and add as much water as is necessary to mix. The more water you add, the longer the drying time.

Adapt the material depending on your end use: add lime, cement, and boric acid to increase the pH, making the papercrete fire-resistant and less attractive to bugs; prickly pear goo and latex paint make it water-resistant; sand adds grit and structure; and clay lets the mix breathe, allowing moisture in and out.

The tools you need are dictated by the volume being produced. Small batches can be made in a 5-gallon bucket and mixed with a mixing paddle attachment on a standard drill. Large batches can be made in a handmade tow-behind mixer, like we did. Papercrete slurry can be pumped with a 9-horsepower trash pump. You can use traditional stucco tools to spread the papercrete. It can also be sprayed with a stucco sprayer (that requires an air compressor).

Imagine a Papercrete Dome

The papercrete dome Mikey and I designed is not hard to build — Mikey and I are not big people, and we did it ourselves without outside help. The process amounts to building a metal armature and filling the walls with papercrete, then mortaring the walls inside and out.

SketchUp is user-friendly shareware that can be downloaded free from the Internet. With it you can draft sophisticated to-scale plans for buildings, projects, and landscaping. We used SketchUp to make a 3-D drawing of our dome. You can use our design — all of our drawings are free online (see Resources, page 308).

If you are building on a cement slab, anchor-bolt metal plates to the slab and attach the dome to these plates with a weld. If you are building on the earth, you'll need to dig a foundation ring that your rebar armature will sit in. We made ours 1 foot deep and 1 foot wide. The first foot of our dome's rebar ladders sits in this ring. The ring is filled with cement to stabilize it.

The rebar armature is done. Each rebar ladder is joined together at the top. It's time to run the electric.

TOOLS FOR PAPERCRETE DOME

REBAR AND ARMATURE
hydraulic rebar cutter
metal chop saw
MIG welder
bolt cutters
dykes
vise grips
drill
handheld wood saw

MORTAR AND PAPER FILL
9-horsepower trash pump
250-gallon tow-behind papercrete
  mixer or bucket mixer
paper (nonglossy preferable)
cement
additives such as lime, boric acid, and
  prickly pear goo (optional)
trowel and hawk

SKINNING THE WALLS
pneumatic hog ring gun
dykes
vise grips
metal lath
metal remesh
metal scissors

*Farming tools have proven
useful for building. Building
a rebar armature went
much faster once we
picked up a pneumatic hog
ring tie that mechanically
attaches the rebar to the
metal lath with a loop
meant to tag a farm hog.*

The armature is made up of rebar ladders welded together and formed on a wooden jig. A wooden jig is just like a small stage — two large pieces of plywood screwed down to a 2-foot by 4-foot frame. Making armature ladders requires drawing out the dome's wall shape on the jig. A hemispherical dome design offers the most headroom and can be achieved by starting the wall's curve at about 6 feet. Use the jig to weld the metal ladders in place. The jig assures that each ladder made is the same size. The number of ladders made depends on the size of the dome. The structural engineer who approves yours will tell you how many she or he thinks is best.

The rebar ladders join at the dome's apex and attach to an ocular (a circle also made out of rebar). When all the ladders are attached to the ocular, rebar hoops are made to fit around the body of the dome and are welded in place 1 foot apart from each other, beginning at ground level and ending at the very top of the dome. Think ring-toss when imagining how these fit the design. These horizontal hoops give the armature support when they're welded to the vertical ladders. At this stage, cut away areas where windows and doors will be placed and cut spaces to mount electrical outlets, light switches, and plumbing. Run electric and plumbing. Window and doorframes can be built out of either metal or wood.

Once this rebar dome is standing, its outer and inner walls are skinned, first with 6-inch remesh and then metal lath. The remesh is hand tied to the rebar with baling wire. The metal lath can be applied with a pneumatic tool called a hog ring tie that works with an air compressor. At this stage the dome looks like a birdcage, with the skinned exterior and interior walls 1 foot apart. This is the space where the papercrete goes. Remesh the interior first so that you can still climb the exterior metal lath while applying remesh to it. Work from the top down.

Before pouring a papercrete wall, consider filling the first 1 foot of the walls with a nonwicking material so that pooled water that

I use a welder to secure loose rebar connections and to weld the electrical boxes into place.

After skinning the dome, we ran the electric and put in the door. Our friend Smoke designs the neon portion of the burning man at each year's festival; his extra parts light our threshold.

follows rain and gathers around the dome's circumference will not wick up inside the walls. Waste materials that are suitable for this purpose include glass bottles and stones — anything nonwicking, abundant, and free.

We mixed our papercrete in a homemade tow-behind mixer that could handle 250-gallon batches. Once mixed, the paper slurry is poured into the walls through a hole made near the top. If you have a trash pump, you have the option of pumping the slurry into the walls. For a tough exterior mortar, increase the recipe's cement portion. For a breathable interior wall, add mud to the mix.

TIPS

- Let dry completely before sealing, or it may attract mold. (Know that papercrete requires a long drying time. Building when there's a good chance of rain isn't a very good idea.)
- Use glass bottles in papercrete walls to let in light. Be sure your windows face south.
- Papercrete is a good insulator; a tiny wood-burning stove can heat a 1,000-square-foot room.

We built our own mixer out of a feed tank, I-beam, and the differential from a Ford 150. When towed by our pickup truck, a blade mounted inside chops the paper and turns it into pulp.

Remodel Existing Buildings

In addition to building papercrete structures, Mikey and I remodeled a 40-year-old mobile home and a 20-foot shipping container that we floored with bamboo, painted, and ran power in. Both the mobile home and the shipping container were waste materials.

Because RVs, trailers, and mobile homes are small, they are easy to work with and inexpensive to remodel. Often they can be obtained for free if you haul them yourself. Because they are smaller than many homes, they do not require a lot of materials or labor. They're not worth a whole lot, so they make good learning projects: mistakes are not expensive. These structures are easily transformed into guesthouses, art studios, and offices.

TIPS

- Working as an apprentice to a skilled builder on your own house reduces labor costs and is a great way to learn about techniques, tools, and materials.
- Remodeling means less permitting, fees, and inspector visits.
- Add extra insulation when remodeling. Look for structures that are south-facing or can be moved to face south. This will reduce heating and cooling costs. Additional windows should always be placed on the south side.
- Find a comfortable place to live while you are building or remodeling a home. It will take longer than you think to finish the work.

Turn a Shipping Container into a Building

Shipping containers, once dented, are unusable for cargo but make fine storage sheds and can be modified into a variety of buildings. They typically come in two lengths: 20-foot by 8-foot and 40-foot by 8-foot, with ⅝-inch marine-grade birch floors.

Companies that specialize in shipping containers are often prepared to provide modified containers with doors, windows, ventilation, power, and plumbing for running water added to them. A good supplier can modify the ends of containers so that they can be fit together and made watertight. Be sure that the modifications you preorder are going to be done by a certified electrician or plumber to avoid future problems passing inspections. Save the pieces of metal that have been cut away to make openings for doors and windows. These can be used for other projects such as gates, fences, and doors (see page 21).

TIPS

- Prepare for delivery by pouring four level concrete footers, one for each corner of the box to sit on. If you live in North America, face the long side of the container and any windows south so that the box will gain heat from the sun during the winter.
- Find a supplier near where you live, because transportation is expensive. Make sure the company has the equipment to properly deliver a shipping container. A flatbed with tilt drop is best and makes for fast delivery and accuracy within 4 inches of your desired location.
- Check the container for smells, dents that may have created a hole, and stains on the floor. Check for rust on the roof and below.
- Refrigerated shipping containers are highly insulated. If you can find one, it will likely cost twice as much as the other containers. It is worth paying a lot extra for one if you plan to spend time in the container. You will make back the money in reduced heating and cooling costs.
- Painting the roof white and shading the structure will reduce heat during the summer months. You can also spray the exterior with

papercrete to deflect some of the sun's heat. Mikey recently framed his shipping container lab with misters that spray the exterior, consuming a couple of gallons of water per hour. This reduces the heat radiating from the metal of the container at peak temperatures midday and provides air conditioning to his lab. We planted grapevines near the misters so that the water being used would not be wasted. The grapes are thriving.

- Well-placed vents — one low to the ground and another placed in the roof — will accommodate airflow during the extremes of winter and summer. A roof turbine ventilator will let hot air out in the summertime but should then be closed up in the winter to keep the heat in.

Mikey loves his shipping container lab and uses it to build all of the electronic devices that we sell in our online store. He still wishes he could bury it in the ground like Luke Skywalker's Tatooine home in Star Wars.

Make Your Home Efficient

Doing two things can noticeably cut your electric power consumption:
- Use a clothesline instead of an electric dryer.
- Switch from an upright refrigerator to a converted chest freezer.

Chest freezers are more efficient than stand-up refrigerators because cold air sinks. When a chest freezer is opened, there is very little loss of temperature. When an upright refrigerator is opened, the cold air inside pours out to the kitchen floor. When the door is closed again, the compressor must turn on to produce more cold air.

Switching from a stand-up refrigerator to a converted chest freezer requires only a temperature controller and a reorientation about how goods are stored in the refrigerator. Plug a chest freezer into a temperature controller set to the desired refrigeration temperature. The closer this is set to freezing, the longer the food inside will last.

Once you've converted, organize plastic bins in various sizes and label them: dairy, vegetables, condiments, produce, and protein. Store goods in their appropriate bin so that they are easy to find. When organizing condiments, read each bottle to see which condiments actually need refrigeration. Most do not and can be stored in a cabinet.

Heat and Cool

Our 40-year-old mobile home has almost no insulation and old, leaky single-pane windows that don't quite close all the way.

In an effort to avoid overinvesting in an old mobile home that has a limited life span, we made heating and cooling part of our lifestyle instead of, for example, replacing the windows with double-pane versions.

The first winter that we lived in our home we set the thermostat at 70°F and forgot about it. The first gas bill we received was $180. Today, when we use these tricks, our bill does not exceed $45 even during the coldest months of winter. Yet we have not added insulation, and we still have the original leaky single-pane windows.

TIPS

- Turn the hot-water heater off (or lower it) in summer.
- Electric space heaters are inefficient and best used only in emergencies.
- Make the most of the sun. During winter at sunrise, open all the east- and south-facing curtains and blinds. As the sun makes its way to the west portion of the sky and begins to come in through your west-facing windows, open those on the west side, too. Just before sunset close up all the curtains and blinds to hold the heat you've gained until the sun rises again in the morning. Keep north windows covered at all times of day.
- In the winter, reduce drafts by closing the doors of unused rooms. In the summer, increase airflow by opening windows on opposite sides of the house (or of a room) just a crack (½ inch). This encourages a pull of air that is felt as movement, a breeze.
- Replacing all the windows in a home is extremely expensive. And, according to an article in *National Geographic*, the energy savings created by switching from single- to double-pane windows is about 10 percent. Do the math: Look at your heating bills, the price of windows, and calculate. Would your savings be worth it?
- White reflects the sun's light and keeps a home cooler. Dark colors absorb the sun's heat and make a home warmer. In warm climates, paint your roof white to decrease summer cooling needs. To warm water using solar energy, paint water tanks black and place them outside.
- If you live in the northern hemisphere, the rooms on the north side of a home are cooler than those on the south side. Use them accordingly, and at the right time of year. Try to let fresh air in from your east windows. They are closest to neutral.

- Adding thermostats to heating and cooling devices reduces heating and cooling costs. Programmable thermostats allow you to reduce energy use at specific times of day, such as when you are asleep or not home. Thermostats also turn things on and off at the right time whether or not you remember.
- In dry climates, swamp coolers cool interiors with four times less energy than air conditioners. Swamp coolers are basically fans that move over water to add humidity to an indoor space. We cool 1,200 square feet of space with a single 300-watt swamp cooler rather than using power-hungry air conditioners.

LAYERED WINDOW COVERINGS

Layering a window with the right materials provides year-round options for heating and cooling. In summer months close up the window coverings before reaching the heat of the day; in winter trap heat by closing them at dusk.

1. Silver Mylar bubble wrap makes an excellent reflective covering for your windows: The sun bounces off it in summer months and in the winter it seals out leaks. Cut a roll of Mylar bubble wrap to match the window's size.

2. With a couple of screws, attach the top end to the window frame.

3. Loop a piece of metal wire through the Mylar halfway down and in the center.

4. Hang a small picture hook in the center top of the window frame. When the Mylar is rolled up, the picture hanger will catch the loop and hold up the Mylar roll.

5. A thin, semitransparent fabric that acts as a light diffuser

comes next. Diffusers let the sun shine into a room while softening the quality of its light and intensity of its heat.

6. For the final layer, use a heavy drape made of a material such as cotton velvet. This layer is best lined with a light color and reflective material. The heavy layer helps close up the house to hold in the heat gained from the sun each day. The semireflective liner helps keep the heat of the sun away from the house in summer months.

Holy scrap

Here are a few projects that exemplify what Mikey and I love to do on our homestead: Rescue what others might throw out, and turn waste into useful and even beautiful things.

TOUGHIE SKATEBOARD

A toughie skateboard can be used to push oversized, heavy, and awkward objects like water totes, water heaters, furniture, and refrigerators.

3-foot by 2-foot scrap of plywood

jigsaw

crayon

a pair of wide, knobby skateboard wheel sets

screws

1. Draw the shape of an extra-wide skateboard body onto your plywood scrap.
2. Cut the shape out using a jigsaw.
3. Attach the wheels to the bottom 6 inches from each end.

FIRE BARREL

Fire connects us to nature, to light and heat. Mobile homes are flammable and fireplaces are not recommended in them, so our outdoor fire pit is where we gather with friends in winter months. We also make decorative fire barrels out of found 50-gallon metal drums (see page 45). We find them more beautiful and interesting than the outdoor fire pits sold in stores. Plus, they're made from free and easily obtained waste material. They're easy to make if you have basic welding skills.

50-gallon metal drum*

oxyacetylene torch setup or plasma cutter

safety gloves

protective eyewear (specifically for welding)

metal tire rim

1. Draw out the barrel's design in advance, considering the effect of what gets cut away. Negative spaces will become holes in the barrel. Too many cuts, or ones too large or too close together, will compromise the barrel's integrity. It will be necessary at times to leave parts of your image connected to the rest of the body; plan for these in advance.

2. Using your torch, remove the top of the barrel so that one end is open. Leave the cylinder and its base.

3. Cut a series of decorative holes, as you like. Make sure your design includes a few holes near the bottom 10 inches of the barrel, because these low cuts will let in the air needed to fuel the fire inside the barrel.

4. After the design has been cut, weld a metal tire rim to the bottom of the barrel in the center. This will be the barrel's base, keeping it off the ground and allowing for good airflow.

*Never use a drum that stored combustible chemicals. Play it safe.

SOLAR WATER HEATER OR DOORMAT

If you see a refrigerator in the trash, use a bolt cutter to chop off the compressor coil, an approximately 2-foot by 4-foot metal grate on the back with tubing running through it. The refrigerant moves through this coil when the refrigerator is working. Once the coil is free from the refrigerator, it can be made into a solar water heater by plumbing it, running water through it, and placing it in the sun. Or a portion the size of a welcome mat can be cut from it and placed in front of the door of your home for removing rocks and dirt from the bottom of shoes before entering.

Our neighbor Donna turned us onto the idea of using old refrigerator coils as doormats. On our way home from the dog park this morning, she dug one out of a pile by a dumpster. We took three more home with us. I immediately grabbed the bolt cutters and trimmed it down to size.

RUST RECOVERY

Rusty tools need not become trash.
A simple process of electrolysis can remove rust.

rusty object in need of salvation

two alligator clips

scrap of steel

5-gallon plastic bucket

water

about 1 cup baking soda

battery charger from any DC home device (such as a plug-in charger for an appliance)

enough white vinegar to cover object

1. Connect one end of an alligator clip to the item you wish to recover (de-rust). Connect the end of the other alligator clip to a piece of scrap steel that you are willing to throw away (it won't be usable after this application). The positive alligator clip goes to the scrap metal, and the negative goes to the item being recovered.

2. Place the recovery item and the scrap steel into a bucket of water and baking soda, with the alligator clips coming out the top.

3. Connect the other ends of the alligator clips to the charging device, the positive end on the positive lead and the negative end on the negative lead. If you are uncertain about which end is positive and which is negative, use a multimeter.

4. Plug the charger in. The water will fizz. Leave this setup running for 8 to 20 hours. To check the progress, unplug the charging device from the wall socket and look at your rusted item.

5. When the item is rust-free, take it out and submerge it in a tub of white vinegar for about an hour.

REMOVE

SAVE THIS RUSTY WRENCH

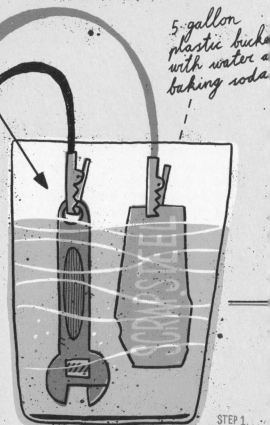

5 gallon plastic bucket with water a baking soda

BATTERY CHARGER OF ANY DC HOME DEVICE

SCRAP STEEL

STEP 1.

ALLIGATOR CLIP (POSITIVE)

ALLIGATOR CLIP (NEGATIVE)

RUST

with electrolysis

saved (RUSTY) WRENCH

STEP 3.

STEP 2.

GARDEN COLANDER

If you see an old washing machine in the trash, grab the basin, the part that the clothes go in. This may require disassembling the unit a bit. Enamel basins in old washing machines are preferable to plastic basins in new machines. Enamel is durable and lasting. Use the basin for an outdoor garden colander for washing large harvests of fruits and vegetables.

PLASTIC WELDING

Broken plastic goods need not go into the trash. Plastic welding is simple — and you only need nail polish remover and some cotton swabs. Seriously.

acetone, a.k.a. nail polish remover (check the bottle for high acetone ratio)

cotton swabs

1. Dip a cotton swab in the acetone and rub both ends of the break in a plastic item with it. Rub back and forth until you feel the plastic soften.

2. Reunite the two ends and hold them together until they bond.

3. When this bond dries, mend the seam by applying more acetone over the seam until you can no longer detect the break.

Epilogue: Make Mistakes

Try again. Fail again. Fail better.
— SAMUEL BECKETT

Mistakes are unavoidable and should therefore be expected when acquiring mad skills. And here's the thing: shared mistakes are valuable.

In that spirit, I'm leaving you with a list of lessons Mikey and I learned the hard way.

Build a workshop first, then build everything else. We were so anxious to remodel our home and property that we began working in spite of not having a workshop. Each day we hauled tools out of our shipping container shed, dragged them to the spot where we were working, unpacked them, set them up, and then each day packed them back up and put them away.

Consider your environment when you make priorities. Mikey and I live in a hot desert with scorching UV rays. Thinking only about house and food, we did not build shade until after remodeling our home and building our gardens. This meant working in the sun, with unnecessary suffering and energy drain.

Allow cement to completely dry before sealing. Wishing to avoid a toxic store-bought product, I stained a cement slab in our yard with natural umber powder that I hydrated. Then I sealed it with a cement sealer. A year later, the slab chipped and I learned what spalling is: it happens when water is sealed into the cement.

Build a humanure system as soon as possible. During the remodeling of our mobile home, we were so committed to using waste and preserving existing materials that we kept the two 40-year-old toilets in the home. I figured that with a bit of elbow grease I could get them clean, but I was wrong. I don't wish that we'd bought new toilets, but I do wish we'd set up a humanure system outdoors and stopped using indoor toilets altogether. Home plumbing can be tricky and expensive to repair. Humanure is a composting toilet that is simple to manage and requires no plumber. Its impact on the environment is much less than flush toilets that waste water.

Watch out for mold spores! While making blue cheese, we learned that mold spores roam free inside buildings. After throwing away a failed batch of blue cheese that smelled like stinky feet, we made a batch of cheddar and noticed that the blue cheese's mold spores had moved over to the cheddar. This time, after throwing away the contaminated cheddar cheese, we scrubbed our cheese fridge and fermentation tank and opened all the windows for a while to clear out the unwanted spores before starting another batch of cheese.

Don't get ahead of yourself and buy batteries before you need them. We were so excited to build our PV solar system that we purchased the batteries a year before installing the system. The batteries sat in our yard while we built a dome to house the inverters and gear. The dome took longer than expected, and the batteries lost resilience sitting in the yard unused. Our batteries' capacity was permanently affected by this loss.

Put what you will need to access in easy-to-reach places. We chose a pole mount for our PV solar panels because the roof of a mobile home is not strong enough to hold a lot of weight. Our PV panels stand at 8 feet above the ground near the roofline of our home. They're too high to access without struggle and are difficult to clean, and their tilt cannot be changed. We cannot maximize their exposure to the sun as it moves through the sky at different times of the year. If we could do it over again, we'd choose to mount them low and in reach, where they could be adjusted. We'd place them on an adjustable mount so that their angle could be changed at different times of the year.

Consider the limits of your chosen materials. We got a little caught up in achieving technical challenges. This was particularly true in our use of papercrete. Papercrete has its uses: it is excellent for insulation and works well in domes. But we should have avoided the backbreaking, time-consuming work of building a solid papercrete slab wall. There are better choices of materials for making a privacy wall. The papercrete slab wall we built also needed a stucco job to withstand time. On the other hand, the fence we made using hollow armature and sprayed papercrete is durable and lasting, especially because we mixed in some prickly pear cactus goo.

Follow nature's rules. Dreaming of an edible landscape in our first two years, we planted many nonindigenous trees. We took risks and planted exotic varieties not from our region. Planting local native trees would have saved us time and energy, and we would have had shade and food faster.

Have fun and play nice. This is hardly a complete list of the mistakes we've made. We suggest you make your own. Making them is more fun than you'd think, and you always learn from them.

RESOURCES

Do, or do not. There is no "try."

— YODA, IN *Star Wars*

These resources are listed by broad topics covered in this book. Within each section you'll find books, websites and blogs, and films (including both YouTube shorts and feature-length movies). Some people warn against using Wiki references, but I think that it's important that we do. We're building the commons. This means using it, relying on it, and contributing to it.

Holy Scrap

HOLY SCRAP
Store. *http://store. holyscraphotsprings.com*
Blog. *http://blog. holyscraphotsprings.com*

MIKEY SKLAR
www.screwdecaf.cx
YouTube. *www.youtube.com/user/ sklarm*
Flickr. *www.flickr.com/ photos/11461247@N02*

WENDY TREMAYNE
www.gaiatreehouse.com

Building

Alexander, Christopher, Sara Ishikawa, Murray Silverstein, Max Jacobson, Ingrid Fiksdahl-King, and Shlomo Angel. *A Pattern Language: Towns, Buildings, Construction.* Oxford University Press, 1977.

Alexander, Christopher. *The Timeless Way of Building.* Oxford University Press, 1979.

Garbage Warrior. Directed by Oliver Hodge. DVD. Open Eye Media Ltd., 2008.

Guelberth, Cedar Rose, and Dan Chiras. *The Natural Plaster Book: Earth, Lime and Gypsum Plasters for Natural Homes.* New Society Publishers, 2003.

McDonough, William, and Michael Braungart. *Cradle to Cradle: Remaking the Way We Make Things.* North Point Press, 2002.

THE ANTTI LOVAG PROJECT
www.anttilovag.org

CAL-EARTH: THE CALIFORNIA INSTITUTE OF ART AND ARCHITECTURE
www.calearth.org

EARTHSHIP BIOTECTURE, LLC
http://earthship.com

EVE'S GARDEN BED AND BREAKFAST
www.evesgarden.org

FERROCEMENT EDUCATIONAL NETWORK
http://ferrocement.net/flist

FLYINGCONCRETE: STRUCTURAL AND SCULPTURAL FORMS IN LIGHTWEIGHT CONCRETE
http://flyingconcrete.com

MORTARSPRAYER.COM
www.mortarsprayer.com. Stucco and texture sprayers

"NADER KHALILI"
Wikipedia. *http://en.wikipedia.org/wiki/Nader_Khalili*

PAPERCRETES: PAPERCRETE INFO
http://groups.yahoo.com/group/papercreters

ROBERT BRUNO
http://robertbruno.com

SPACEMAN'S PAPERCRETE MIXER
www.starship-enterprises.net/Papercrete/Mixer

Emergent Culture

THE BEEHIVE DESIGN COLLECTIVE
www.beehivecollective.org

BILLIONAIRES FOR BUSH
www.billionairesforbush.com

BLACK ROCK ARTS FOUNDATION
http://blackrockarts.org

"BOING BOING"
www.boingboing.net

BURNING MAN
www.burningman.com

CULT OF LESS
http://cultofless.com

THE LONG NOW FOUNDATION
http://longnow.org

MADAGASCAR INSTITUTE
www.madagascarinstitute.com

MAKER FAIRE
http://makerfaire.com

"PIRATE PARTY"
Wikipedia. *http://en.wikipedia.org/ wiki/Pirate_Party*

RADIOLAB
New York Public Radio. *www.radiolab.org*

REVEREND BILLY AND THE CHURCH OF STOP SHOPPING
www.revbilly.com

WORK LESS PARTY
www.worklessparty.org

Friends/Blogs We Like

ALYCE SANTORO: CENTER FOR THE IMPROBABLE & (IM)PERMACULTURAL RESEARCH
www.alycesantoro.com

ART IS THE PROPER TASK OF LIFE
http://artisthepropertaskoflife. blogspot.com

CAMERON, HEATHER
True Stitches (blog). *http://truestitches. blogspot.com*

THE COMMON MILKWEED
http://thecommonmilkweed.blogspot. com

THE ESSENTIAL HERB BLOG
http://theessentialherbal.blogspot.com

GROWING HEART FARM
http://growingheartfarm.com

HESS, ANNA AND MARK HAMILTON
http://blog.homemadespaceship.net

HOMEMADE SPACESHIP
http://blog.homemadespaceship.net

IRIS HERBAL
www.irisherbal.com

LAZULI, GIANNI (FLUXROSTRUM)
Fluxview, USA (blog). *http://fluxview.com/USA*

LUKE ISEMAN
http://lukeiseman.com

OLD MONTICELLO ORGANIC FARMS
http://oldmonticelloorganicfarms.com

REINISH, LIBBY
Whittled Down (blog).
www.whittleddown.com

SHIVA, VANDANA
www.navdanya.org

VELA CREATIONS
www.velacreations.com

ZIELINSKI, JULIE, AND ERIC WILSON
d.i. wine & dine (blog). *http://di-wineanddine.blogspot.com*

Gift Economy and the Commons

Hyde, Lewis. *Common as Air: Revolution, Art, and Ownership.* Farrar, Straus and Giroux, 2010.

———. *The Gift: Imagination and the Erotic Life of Property.* Vintage Books, 1983.

Lessig, Lawrence. *The Future of Ideas: The Fate of the Commons in a Connected World.* Vintage Books, 2002.

CREATIVE COMMONS
http://creativecommons.org

FREE SOFTWARE FOUNDATION
www.fsf.org

GITHUB, INC
https://github.com

ON THE COMMONS
www.onthecommons.org

OPEN SOURCE ECOLOGY
http://opensourceecology.org

WIKILEAKS
www.wikileaks.org

DIY/Tutorials

Adkins, Jan. *Moving Heavy Things.* WoodenBoat Publications, 2004.

Tresemer, David Ward. *The Scythe Book: Mowing Hay, Cutting Weeds, and Harvesting Small Grains with Hand Tools,* 2nd ed. A. C. Hood, 1996.

ADAFRUIT INDUSTRIES
http://adafruit.com

AFRIGADGET
www.afrigadget.com

DORKBOT
http://dorkbot.org

HACK A DAY
http://hackaday.com

"HACKERSPACES"
HackerspaceWiki. *http://hackerspaces.org/wiki*

INSTRUCTABLES
www.instructables.com

MAKE: CRAFT
http://blog.makezine.com/craftzine

MAKE: MAGAZINE
http://makezine.com

SWAP-O-RAMA-RAMA
www.swaporamarama.org

TRIMBLE SKETCHUP
www.sketchup.com

Fuel

FILLUP4FREE.COM
http://fillup4free.com
Home of the Waste Vegetable Oil Network Map

SKLAR, MIKEY
"DIY Biodiesel: 5 Minute Microbatches."
YouTube. *www.youtube.com/watch?v=LdHPbVh38SM*

Lifestyle

Bay Laurel, Alicia. *Living on Earth.* Vintage Books, 1971.

Jenkins, Joseph. *The Humanure Handbook: A Guide to Composting Human Manure,* 3rd ed. Chelsea Green Publishing, 2005.

Nearing, Helen, and Scott Nearing. *Living the Good Life: How to Live Sanely and Simply in a Troubled World.* Schocken, 1970. Originally published in 1954.

No Impact Man. Directed Laura Gabbert and Justin Schein. DVD. Oscilloscope Pictures, 2009.

Steinfeld, Carol. *Liquid Gold: The Lore and Logic of Using Urine to Grow Plants.* Green Frigate Books, 2004.

Plants: Food & Medicine

Amrein-Boyes, Debra. *200 Easy Homemade Cheese Recipes.* R. Rose, 2009.

Bittman, Mark. "Bad Food? Tax It." *New York Times,* July 24, 2011.

Cech, Richo. *Making Plant Medicine.* Horizon Herbs, 2000.

Desert Harvesters. *Eat Mesquite!: A Cookbook.* Green Press Initiative, 2011.

Ivey, Robert DeWitt. *Flowering Plants of New Mexico.* RD&V Ivey, 2003.

Kane, Charles W., and Frank Rose. *Herbal Medicine of the American Southwest.* Lincoln Town Press, 2006.

Katz, Sandor Ellix. *The Art of Fermentation: An In-Depth Exploration of Essential Concepts and Processes from Around the World.* Chelsea Green, 2012.

———. *Wild Fermentation: The Flavor, Nutrition, and Craft of Live-Culture Foods.* Chelsea Green, 2003.

Knishinsky, Ran. *Prickly Pear Cactus Medicine: Treatments for Diabetes, Cholesterol, and the Immune System.* Healing Arts Press, 2004.

Lowenfels, Jeff, and Wayne Lewis. *Teaming with Microbes: A Gardener's Guide to the Soil Food Web.* Timber Press, 2006.

Moore, Michael. *Medicinal Plants of the Mountain West,* rev. ed. Museum of New Mexico Press, 2003.

Neithammer, Carolyn. *American Indian Cooking: Recipes from the Southwest.* University of Nebraska Press, 1999. First published as *American Indian Food and Lore* by Macmillan, 1974.

Phyo, Ani. *Ani's Raw Food Essentials.* Da Capo Press, 2010.

Pollan, Michael. *The Botany of Desire: A Plant's-Eye View of the World.* Random House, 2001.

———. *In Defense of Food: An Eater's Manifesto.* Penguin, 2008.

———. *The Omnivore's Dilemma.* Penguin, 2006.

Rose, Jeanne. *Herbal Body Book,* 2nd ed. Frog, Ltd., 2000.

Stamets, Paul. *Mycelium Running: How Mushrooms Can Help Save the World.* Ten Speed Press, 2005.

DESERT HARVESTERS
www.desertharvesters.org

NATIONAL YOUNG FARMERS' COALITION
www.youngfarmers.org

ORGANIC CONSUMERS ASSOCIATION
www.organicconsumers.org

Power/Energy

Chase, Jon. "The Grouse: Assault on Batteries." *Popular Science,* January 29, 2008.

Solar Energy International. *Photovoltaics: Design and Installation Manual.* New Society Publishers, 2004.

DIY SOLAR OVEN
DIY Solar Network. *http://diysolar. dasolar.com/group/diysolaroven*

SKLAR, MIKEY
"PV Solar (Off-Grid)." YouTube. *www. youtube.com/watch?v=Seaw5S3lhSs*

Philosophy

Fadiman, James and Robert Frager, eds. *Essential Sufism*. HarperCollins, 1997.

Gandhi, Mahatma. *The Essential Writings of Mahatma Gandhi*. Edited by Raghavan Narasimhan. Iyer. Oxford University Press, 1993.

Inayat Khan, Hazrat. *Complete Works of Pir-o-Murshid Hazrat Inayat Khan*. East-West Publishers, 1996.

Inayat-Khan, Pir Zia. *The Holy Mysteries of the Five Elements*, 2nd ed. Sufi Order International Publications, 2008.

Meyer, Wali Ali; Bilal Hyde; Faisal Muqaddam; and Shabda Kahn. *Physicians of the Heart: A Sufi View of the Ninety-nine Names of Allah*. Sufi Ruhaniat International, 2011.

Novalis. *The Novices of Sais*. Translated by Ralph Manheim. Archipelago, 2005.

Steiner, Rudolf. *Nature's Open Secret: Introductions to Goethe's Scientific Writings*. Anthroposophic, 2000.

THE ABODE OF THE MESSAGE
www.theabode.org

COUNCIL FOR A PARLIAMENT OF THE WORLD'S RELIGIONS
www.parliamentofreligions.org

SEVEN PILLARS HOUSE OF WISDOM
www.sevenpillarshouse.org

SULUK ACADEMY
http://sulukacademy.org

Water

Evenari, Michael; Leslie Shanan; and Naphtali Tadmor. *The Negev: the Challenge of a Desert*, 2nd ed. Harvard University Press, 1982.

Flow: For Love of Water. Directed by Irena Salina. DVD. Oscilloscope Pictures, 2008.

Lancaster, Brad. *Rainwater Harvesting for Drylands*. 2 vols. Rainsource Press, 2006–2008.

Ludwig, Art. *Water Storage: Tanks, Cisterns, Aquifers, and Ponds*. Oasis Design, 2005.

World Condition

The Corporation. Directed by Mark Achbar and Jennifer Abbot. DVD. Zeitgeist Films, 2004.

A Crude Awakening: The Oil Crash. Directed by Basil Gelpke and Ray McCormack. DVD. Lava Productions, 2006.

Eisenstein, Charles. *The Ascent of Humanity.* Panenthea Press, 2007.

End of Suburbia: Oil Depletion and the Collapse of The American Dream. Director Gregory Greene. DVD. The Electric Wallpaper Co., 2004.

Food, Inc. Directed by Robert Kenner. Magnolia Pictures, 2008.

An Inconvenient Truth: A Global Warning. Directed by Davis Guggenheim. DVD. Paramount Home Entertainment, 2006.

King Corn. Directed by Aaron Woolf. Mosaic Films Inc., 2007.

McKibben, Bill. "Politics: Global Warming's Terrifying New Math." *Rolling Stone.* July 19, 2012.

Rushkoff, Douglas. *Life Inc.: How the World Became a Corporation and How to Take It Back.* Random House, 2009.

Wilson, Peter Lamborn; Christopher Bamford; and Kevin Townley. *Green Hermeticism: Alchemy and Ecology.* Lindisfarne Books, 2007.

Wolf, Naomi. *The End of America: Letter of Warning to a Young Patriot.* Chelsea Green Publishing, 2007.

Zeitgeist: The Movie. Directed by Peter Joseph. GMP, 2007.

Zinn, Howard. *A People's History of the United States: 1492–present,* 20th anniversary ed. HarperCollins, 2005.

CARBON TRACKER INITIATIVE
www.carbontracker.org

CORPORATE CRIME REPORTER
www.corporatecrimereporter.com

INFLUENCE EXPLORER
www.influenceexplorer.com

JAMES HOWARD KUNSTLER
www.kunstler.com

NAOMI KLEIN
www.naomiklein.org

POST CARBON INSTITUTE
www.postcarbon.org

TRUTHDIG
www.truthdig.com

THE YES MEN
http://theyesmen.org

ACKNOWLEDGMENTS

Loving thanks to my partner in life, Mikey Sklar, for weaving a magic carpet that I rode safely into my own dreams. Thank you to Pir Zia Inayat-Khan, my ideal. I thank you for showing me the way to travel, and for sharing the tools that led me to love the life of this world. To Tony Rubin, thank you for treasuring me. To the vibrant community in Truth or Consequences, New Mexico, thanks for generosity of heart, friendship, community, and for welcoming Mikey and me into your family. Special thanks to Yarrow and Megan at the Little Sprout, Rhonda at the Black Cat, Jessica at Bella Luca, and all the folks at the Happy Belly Deli for providing great spaces for me to write this book and good company when procrastination was unavoidable. Sincere thanks to Susan Dunlap, Jodi Morgan

Pantuck, Melissa McKinstry, Mina Lebitz, Mary Rose Bennett, Linda Greenberg, and Cheryl Ray for helping me find and shape my words as this manuscript came together. Thank you to Tara Sklar for advice from the other side of the globe. For believing in us as we took real chances, I thank my family and Mikey's. My heartfelt thanks go to the wonderful people who live at the Abode and to the teachers of the Suluk Academy — Maliaka Julie Serrano, Gayan Macher, and Taj Inayat Khan — for the ease that followed their guidance.

Heartfelt thanks to Dale Dougherty, Christopher Bamford, Brad Lancaster, Sandor Ellix Katz, Alyce Santoro, Billy Talen, and Doug Rushkoff for imagining a better world and having the courage, imagination and determination to create it. Your leads gave me the inspiration to do the same. I treasure the words you gave to this book.

I am deeply grateful to the thousands of people who have volunteered creative energy to Swap-O-Rama-Rama, NO bUSH, and the Vomitorium, as well as other projects I produced while discovering a decommodified life. It has been a delight to create a world with you.

Thanks to all the great folks at Burning Man for creating the ground to materialize the myth of Atlantis in our modern age. Thanks to Black Rock Arts Foundation for supporting Swap-O-Rama-Rama in its beginnings and to the producers of the Maker Faire, and *Craft* and *Make* magazines for working tirelessly to usher in a world for makers of things.

I thank all the good people at Storey Publishing, with a special note for my editor, Pam Thompson, whom I thank for her kindheartedness and keen ability to sense what I most wished to express with this work. Thanks to Alethea Morrison for the creativity she generously gave to these pages. I thank the many illustrators who enlivened this book with their own imaginations.

I offer my deepest appreciation to all who conceive of and try to usher in a world freed of money.

— *Wendy Tremayne*
